What Others Have to Say...

Fundraising for All *is excellent. I love its clarity, simplicity, completeness, humor, authenticity, and relatable approach! It does not talk down to the reader; instead, it lifts up the fundraising professional, whether neophyte or veteran.* **—Ann W. Cramer, Sr. Consultant, Coxe Curry and Associates**

Fundraising for All *truly lives up to its title and hits the mark! It accomplishes something remarkable by being both an accessible and digestible introduction to development for a newcomer as well as a deeply useful reference resource for an experienced advancement professional. It will live on my desk and quickly become dog-eared!* **—Brien Lewis, President, Transylvania University**

The most important and difficult job in any nonprofit is raising money. This book gives readers a step-by-step roadmap for preparing a successful fundraising campaign: what to do, how to do it, and specific examples that bring the tasks to life. **—Spring Asher is the co-author, along with Wicke Chambers, of *Wooing and Winning Business: The Foolproof Formula for Making Persuasive Business Presentations***

Fundraising for All *shares a wealth of insights and practical tips that form an essential roadmap for nonprofit executives, development staff, and board members.* **—Laura T. McCarty, President, Georgia Humanities**

Fundraising for All: What Every Fundraising Leader Should Know *is an expansive, easy-to-read how-to manual for a very complex subject. The authors approach this critical function with plain language, humor, and wisdom. They give readers confidence that they, too, can master the revenue side of nonprofit management.* **—Brent Pease, Executive Director, the Kyle Pease Foundation**

Fundraising For All *is destined to become a classic in the field! Her personal storytelling makes for some super-engaging reading. I love the way the book takes complicated issues and offers simple, practical, hands-on solutions. The brilliant tips spread generously across the pages are spot on. I especially enjoyed the revelation that rehearsal is not just for actors, followed by guidance that seems like it was crafted just for me. I can put this to use TODAY! Thanks, Linda and team, for such a beautiful tool to accelerate fundraising success!* **—M. Kent Stroman, CFRE, President, Stroman & Associates**

An essential tool that any non-profit CEO or development professional can use to assess current development strategies and practices. It has the rare combination of both basic development hygiene and sophisticated techniques based on deep practical experience. **—Sheffield Hale, President & CEO, The Atlanta History Center**

Fundraising for All

for All

What Every Nonprofit Leader Should Know

Linda Wise McNay, PhD
Ailena Gibby Parramore
David M. Paule

Fundraising for All: What Every Nonprofit Leader Should Know

Published by Our Fundraising Search

ISBN Print Book: 978-0-578-97413-2

Library of Congress Control Number: 2021917048

13 12 11 10 9 8 7 6 5 4 3 2 1

About the Authors

Linda Wise McNay, PhD

Linda Wise McNay is the founder, owner, and principal consultant with Our Fundraising Search in Atlanta. She has completed more than fifteen years of consulting and has served more than 175 clients. Linda's nonprofit background includes work with higher and secondary education, the arts, human services, and faith-based organizations. It has included work in capital campaigns, annual fund, planned giving, membership, development, and executive search.

Before launching Our Fundraising Search, Linda served as the Chief Development Officer for the High Museum of Art, leading its efforts to raise $95 million to bring great art from the Louvre and China to the Atlanta community. She also managed an endowment campaign, initiated the institution's first full-time planned giving effort, and increased the museum's membership to a record fifty thousand. During her High Museum tenure, Linda served as national president of AMDA, the Art Museum Development Association.

Linda served as Director of Advancement at Pace Academy, a K-12 private school in Atlanta. She led the school's largest and most successful capital fundraising campaign, with a goal of $15 million. The campaign reached its goal ahead of schedule and under budget; and achieved 95 percent parent participation, 100 percent board participation, and 100 percent faculty/staff participation.

In higher education, Linda held positions including Vice President of the Georgia Foundation for Independent Colleges, Executive Director of the Emory Challenge Fund at Emory University, Director of Development at the Georgia Institute of Technology, and alumni and development roles at her alma mater, Transylvania University.

She has been a member of the Association of Fundraising Professionals (AFP) for more than thirty years. Her volunteer work with AFP includes serving as a mentor in the Diversity Fellows Program, serving on the National Philanthropy Day Steering Committee, and serving as Past-Honoree Chair for many years.

Linda wrote three books for nonprofit practitioners: *Fundraising for Schools: 8 Keys to Success Every Head of School Should Know, Fundraising for Museums: 8 Keys to Success Every Museum Leader Should Know,* and *Fundraising for Churches: 12 Keys to Success Every Church Leader Should Know* co-authored with Sarah B. Matthews, with whom she also co-created an online course based on the book.

Linda is dedicated to raising the next generation of philanthropists, co-authoring a children's book, *The Adventures of PhilAnThropy,* with fellow passionate fundraisers Ailena Gibby Parramore and Del Martin.

She is a regular speaker and presenter at workshops and conferences and author of numerous articles for publication. Her doctoral dissertation was entitled, "The Relative Cost-Effectiveness of Three Direct Mail Techniques on Non-Alumni Prospects."

Linda earned her Doctorate in Philosophy of Higher Education from Georgia State University, a Master of Business Administration specializing in Personnel Administration from the University of Kentucky, and a Bachelor of Arts degree from Transylvania University in Lexington, Kentucky. Linda and her architect husband, Gary, have two adult sons.

In her spare time, Linda likes traveling to new places with family and friends, reading, writing, walking, and playing board games.

Ailena Gibby Parramore

Ailena Gibby Parramore has raised millions of dollars for organizations in several arenas since starting her nonprofit journey in 2005. Ailena's background includes work in secondary education, health and human services, and city government. She has experience in departmental planning/structure, annual and capital campaign development and implementation, donor identification, cultivation and stewardship, volunteerism, mass-market special events, and corporate engagement and sponsorships.

Before joining Our Fundraising Search, Ailena served as Director of Development for North Cobb Christian School, a private school in North Metro Atlanta. She reintroduced the annual fund, realizing tremendous growth in financial contributions and strong volunteer leadership. She led the school's largest capital fundraising campaign and its first major gifts campaign for debt reduction, where she was instrumental in securing its first significant foundation gifts. Under her leadership, the campaigns were completed seven and ten months (respectively) ahead of schedule.

During her tenure at the National Multiple Sclerosis Society, Georgia Chapter, Ailena served as the Walk MS, then Bike MS Managers, before becoming the Director of Special Events overseeing the state's largest charity bicycling series (1,800 participants) as well as their series of nine walks across the state. In this role, Ailena oversaw the planning and execution of these mass-market events, including corporate engagement and sponsorship, marketing and promotions, participant/team recruitment and cultivation, logistics, and volunteer management and community engagement. During Ailena's tenure, the chapter saw record-setting increases in Bike MS and Walk MS participation and corporate engagement and sponsorships. Ailena was nominated to serve as the National Marketing Liaison for the Southeast Region and served as the Southeast Region Bike MS Workgroup chair.

While serving the Atlanta City Council President's Office, Ailena held the unique roles of media relations for one of the city's most high-profile leaders and constituent services, which gave her great insight into the complex workings of city government.

Ailena has co-authored a children's book, *The Adventures of PhilAnThropy*. She received her Bachelor of Arts degree in journalism (A.B.J.) with an emphasis in advertising and a minor in psychology from the University of Georgia. She and her husband, Chad, have a son, Taylor, and a daughter, Ella, who keep them very busy. In her spare time, Ailena loves arts and crafts, traveling, and reading.

David M. Paule

Dave Paule is an experienced chief executive officer, fundraiser, marketer, writer, and educator with a track record of accomplishments in strategic planning, marketing communications, product development, branding, e-commerce, and project management. He specializes in jumpstarting stagnant operations, global business turnarounds, and building green-field organizations. He joined Our Fundraising Search as Senior Consultant in 2020.

He is also a member of the faculty of Georgia State University's J. Mack Robinson School of Business, where he teaches the Managerial Sciences curriculum and serves as a member of the Diverse Faculty Alliance and the chair of GSU's PRISM Faculty Identity Group.

Most recently, Dave served as the Executive Director & CEO of The Georgia Lions Lighthouse Foundation ("The Lighthouse"), a nonprofit organization dedicated to preserving vision and hearing in Georgia and the Southeast by providing vision examinations, glasses, and hearing aids to more than twenty-five thousand uninsured and underinsured patients each year. He professionalized its business operations after a significant financial fraud perpetrated by the previous CEO. He was also able to restore the organization to consistent, net-positive financial performance of 5 to 7 percent annually through a combination of strategic revenue management, improved fundraising, and reasonable cost controls. Most significantly, under his leadership, the organization made important advances in the field of optical telemedicine that enabled it to take eye care to Georgia's underserved counties and populations.

Dave worked at Delta Air Lines for most of his career, retiring in 2011 as marketing head for Delta Cargo, the company's $1.1 billion airfreight division. He led product and brand integration in the merger with Northwest Airlines, achieving $60 million in annualized synergies. While at Delta, he held roles in engineering, finance, marketing, and supply chain.

Before joining The Lighthouse, Dave led GreenLaw, an environmental public interest law firm. Previously, he spent two years as Chief Revenue Officer of the Atlanta Opera, where he led the marketing, communications, and fundraising functions and increased overall revenue by 55 percent. He previously served as the Vice President & Chief Marketing Officer for the Atlanta Symphony Orchestra, where he overhauled the promotion, sales, and revenue management functions.

Dave serves on the boards for Callanwolde Fine Art Center, Prevent Blindness Georgia, and the Suzi Bass Awards. He also serves on the Board of Ambassadors for the Grady Foundation.

In his spare time, he is a writer, publishing books and stories under the name D.M.Paule. He released *The Monarch of Key West* in 2001, *Highlands-a-Go-Go: Finding Virginia Highland* in 2009, and *The CEO's Due Diligence Handbook* in 2018.

He also dabbles in photography, broadcasting, video production, and standup comedy.

He holds a Master of Business Administration from Georgia State University and a Bachelor of Science in Aerospace Engineering from the University of Cincinnati. He lives in Atlanta.

Dedication

This book is dedicated to the nonprofit organizations and leaders who understand the importance of ensuring the sustainability of their missions. Our clients—past, present, and future—come to us for help, wisdom, expertise, and (occasionally) therapy. With them in mind, we created this guide.

Authors' Acknowledgments

If you ever want to test the compatibility of co-workers, suggest they write a book together. In our case, all three of us have big personalities. Fortunately, we rose to the occasion. Aside from pitched battles over the Oxford comma, dogmatic interpretations of the *Chicago Manual of Style,* and radically differing opinions on structuring a biography, we all agreed on the fundamentals of what is important about the topic.

Agreeing and writing it down is one thing. Making it into a book is something different. We want to thank the following individuals who accompanied us on this journey:

- Our intern, Davon Holmes, who, in his first professional gig, had the formidable task of trying to get a word in edgewise in staff meetings;

- Holly Hanchey, our editor, who moved mountains and commas (and mountains of commas) to make our deadline;

- Ian McNay, our long-suffering IT support, digital marketing manager, and keeper of critical passwords; and

- Stephen Nill, our book coach, who came back into the ring for a fourth round.

As we discussed in the Dedication, we also thought that we should thank the people who taught us the most about fundraising:

Ailena thanks Linda McNay (yes, her co-author!) for taking a chance on her all those years ago; for recognizing this fish out of water for her skills-to-be in individual giving; for becoming her professional, and many times personal, mentor; for allowing her to reinvent herself at Our Fundraising Search; for taking on the writing of two books together; and ultimately, for her friendship.

Dave thanks Sandy Smith, who hired him straight out of Delta Air Lines and set him on a ten-year nonprofit journey. (She also christened that journey with a vodka or two.)

Linda thanks Jake B. Shrum. She had the privilege of working with him in development at Emory University, before he was president of not one but three colleges. In addition to agreeing to write encouraging words for this book, he makes whoever he is talking to feel like the most important person in the room—a great skill for any fundraiser.

We hope you not only find this book useful but that you enjoy the journey as much as we have.

Contents

Foreword

Fundraising for All is as comprehensive as any book available on how to practice fundraising. Raising funds for nonprofit organizations is more difficult than most of us think, but having a "how to" book about what to do, when to do it, and who should do it, gives its readers a clear path to fundraising success.

No books I have read about fundraising in the last forty-five years have captured the essence of basic fundraising principals as has Fundraising for All. It should be a reference guide for anyone interested in starting, building, and maintaining a successful fundraising program.

Some fundraising books are historic in the field; others are more inspiring. Yet, if I could have only one "how to do fundraising" book on my shelf, I would choose Fundraising for All!

Jake B. Schrum

Jake B. Schrum is an educational administrator with almost fifty years of experience in higher educational fundraising. He learned the craft at Yale University before becoming Vice President for Development at Emory University. He also served as President of Texas Wesleyan University, Southwestern University, and Emory & Henry College.

Editor of *A Board's Guide to Comprehensive Campaigns,* Schrum served as the Chair of CASE International, the Council for the Advancement and Support of Education. In addition, he taught, for five years, the fundraising course at the Harvard Institute for New Presidents.

Schrum absolutely believes that philanthropy can change the world for the sake of humankind.

Introduction

Welcome to the world of fundraising. As a nonprofit leader, you must always keep your eye on revenue production. If your career has followed the example of other nonprofit leaders, while you may have fundraising experience, your path to leadership probably emphasized other elements of your organization's mission. This book was written for you.

"Nonprofit" is a tax status. It is not a license to lose money. The universal laws of gravity and economics apply equally to all: you must produce at least as much as you consume. And yet, we find that most nonprofit leaders and boards have, at best, a rudimentary understanding of earned and contributed revenue. That's why we exist. Our company believes that the best way for nonprofits to achieve their missions is by helping them build sustainable revenue models.

Every nonprofit organization needs to raise money. This includes annual operating support as well as capital and endowment for buildings and maintenance. Following the COVID-19 pandemic, fundraising for nonprofits is even more critical. Those nonprofits that had provided good stewardship in the past and have a reserve fund or endowment will be in better shape than those that have not done so.

This book is a basic "how-to" for any nonprofit leader who may not be experienced in basic fundraising concepts. We present the information in ten chapters in an easy-to-read format, with examples from nonprofits in every sector.

Why *this* fundraising book as opposed to any other? Said simply, it is because we've made the same journey. We've been fundraising leaders, executive directors, and CEOs. We've worked in the arts, education, museums, the environment, and healthcare. Our clients have come across an even broader spectrum of nonprofits. And, we don't mince words. We know you don't have time for elaborate prose.

We believe that fundraising is a team sport and everyone's job, but our book is written with leaders, executives, and boards in mind. Chapters include crafting a compelling case for support, enlisting strong, committed leadership, and drafting and executing a written fundraising plan to support the organization's strategic plan. We provide you with solicitation letters, timetables, and scripts to use in your own fundraising endeavors.

We share best budgeting practices and methods of giving and encourage readers to focus on soliciting major gifts from individuals. In this straightforward book, we provide everything you need to know about fundraising. Included is a bonus chapter on fundraising for young people.

By the time you have finished reading Fundraising for All, you will have a clear understanding of how to raise meaningful dollars, and you will have the confidence to launch a highly successful fundraising campaign. Whether you are head of an organization with total responsibility for fundraising or fortunate to have a chief development officer and a fundraising team, or a board member who wants to support your favorite organization's fundraising activities, this book is for you. If we have forgotten anything, please let us know. We would love to hear from you about your successes and any lingering questions. Happy fundraising!

Know Your Terminology

Advancement: A discipline within education similar to development and fundraising. It encompasses alumni relations, communications, development, and marketing and is an integrated method of managing relationships to encourage philanthropy.

Affinity: The degree to which a donor or prospect has an interest in or passion for an organization's mission.

Capacity: An evaluation of the size of donation a donor has the financial wherewithal to make.

Constituents: The people and businesses with which your organization maintains a relationship. Constituents include donors, volunteers, prospects, and staff. Clients served by the organization, such as patients, subscribers, beneficiaries, etc., can also be considered constituents.

Cultivation: The sum total of the relationship-building activities with donors and prospects to foster their connection to the mission and make a gift.

Development: The process of creating and enhancing relationships with current and potential donors to ensure current and future funding. It is more complex than pure fundraising. Fundraising is primarily about income generation.

Donor: An individual or organization that gives money, goods, or services to an organization. Donors can be individuals, institutions such as foundations or corporations, or other organizations. They differ from sponsors in that they receive nothing in return for their donations.

Moves Management: Donor development and engagement. It is the process by which a current or prospective donor is moved from cultivation to solicitation. "Moves" are the actions an organization takes to bring in donors, establish and improve relationships, and renew contributions.

Prospect: A person or organization that can become a donor but is not yet one. Prospects are evaluated based on both *affinity* and *capacity*.

Prospecting: The act of finding potential donors through meetings, research, and evaluating the support strategies of similar organizations. It is typically the first step in a donor relationship.

Solicitation: Asking the donor for a gift. The solicitation is based on information gleaned from the donor or prospect during cultivation and is for a specific amount and a specific purpose or goal.

Sponsors: Someone who gives money in exchange for some benefit. That benefit could be advertising, entertainment, or other forms of potentially monetizable recognition.

Stewardship: Stewardship is the relationship management process with a donor following a gift and (hopefully) leading up to a subsequent gift. Donors should be thanked for their contributions and then periodically informed how their donations were used and the resulting positive impact.

Suspects: While not a usual term in fundraising, suspects are potential donors that have not yet been researched. Suspects are quickly evaluated to determine whether or not you will advance them to prospects.

Chapter One

It Starts with a Strategic Plan

IN THIS CHAPTER

- ···→ Every nonprofit organization needs a strategic plan.

- ···→ The strategic plan and fundraising plan are closely related.

- ···→ The process does not need to be complicated.

It is logical to ask why we are starting a fundraising book talking about strategic planning. A nonprofit's strategic plan is foundational to the development plan. Every fundraiser needs to be able to answer two questions donors are going to ask:

1. How are you going to use my donation?

2. How will that help the organization achieve its mission?

If the organization does not have a strategic plan that explicitly addresses those questions, the document is not serving its purpose.

Some nonprofit leaders will tell you that strategic plans are simply a box you must check for foundations; others will tell you they are overrated. We argue that they are an essential tool for every organization and leader. They are not, however, a panacea. A strategic plan is not a substitute for good governance, strong leadership, and basic business sense. Rather, the four should work in harmony to help a nonprofit navigate towards its goals.

We like to use a sailing metaphor when explaining strategic plans to boards. Traveling by boat can be a more difficult proposition than traveling on land. Wind, waves, and other vessels' wakes are forces for which you must constantly compensate as you navigate. Similarly, the idea of setting a course then anticipating and compensating for as many opposing forces as possible is the inherent value of a strategic plan for any organization.

Fundraising is the art of the relationship. As fundraisers, we are the most specialized form of salespeople. We "sell" a relationship with an organization. As stated above, donors (especially institutional donors) expect you to articulate how you use their funds and the impact those funds have. Many will make you issue reports documenting that impact. A few things will make a strategic plan valuable for running the organization and communicating that value to donors.

A Good Strategic Plan Will Provide Clarity of Intent Through Clarity of Language

While board and staff may believe they know what the organization is doing—or should be doing—forcing them to articulate it requires them to think about it. More importantly, the process of assembling language around a concept requires the key stakeholders to (hopefully) come to an agreement over the organization's strategy. This is where a key facilitator with good active listening skills is critical. It is not uncommon for two players in a strategic planning process to say diametrically opposite things and then attempt to discharge potential conflict by saying, "we're saying the same thing." A good strategic planning facilitator does not permit this.

The strategic plan must not allow vagaries in the name of courtesy. Instead, it must clearly articulate for those inside and outside the organization what the organization should be doing and why.

A Good Strategic Plan Will Create a Set of Measurements to Evaluate Your Progress and Help Adjust Your Course

Let's return to our sailing metaphor. Crosswinds and waves usually conspire to push a boat off course. By monitoring the winds and waves and the position of the boat, a good sailor can adjust the heading to maximize the efficiency of travel to the destination. On the other hand, without monitoring conditions and evaluating its position, the boat can wind up off course. In the worst-case scenario, it can wind up someplace from which it cannot easily return.

> **When the Plan is not a Plan**
>
> Dave recalls assuming leadership of a failing organization and being handed its strategic plan. It was neither strategic nor a plan. It was simply a document of platitudes. Everything was in there except "Prepare to meet thy God" and "Employees must wash hands before returning to work."
>
> A strategic plan has a limited shelf life, usually three to five years. At a minimum, it must document as measurable goals what the organization will accomplish during that period, how it will achieve those goals, and how it will pay for them.

A strategic plan without a clear set of measurements is nothing more than an aspirational statement. To be useful, the plan must distinguish the organization's results measurements from its process measurements. In turn, the organization's leadership can use these measurements to decide if the organization is off-course, whether there is a more efficient way to get to the destination, and, occasionally, if there is an even better destination.

Results and Process Measurements

Results measurements are an organization's metrics that are directly tied to its mission. Examples might be constituents served, the number of lives improved, or students' average academic performance. They are always measurable and quantifiable and are what you report to show donors that you are using their money in the manner you committed. Results measurements are typically reported to the board of directors and used to hold management accountable.

Process measurements are an organization's metrics that indicate whether the organization is on track to meet its goals and generate the results to which it has committed. They are the metrics that let you identify problems ahead of time. Management typically uses these metrics to run the organization, but they are generally not reported to the board of directors.

A good strategic plan is not a covenant with God. There is no way to anticipate every hurdle the organization could encounter. Nevertheless, anticipating the ones it is likely to encounter frees up resources when the unexpected occurs.

The Best Strategic Plans Provide Management with Both Guidelines and Permission to Say "No"

One of the best things about a well-written strategic plan is that it gives both management and the board clear guidelines to pick and prioritize work. While fundraisers tend to be inherently optimistic, we believe that unbridled optimism is the enemy of effectiveness. As a nonprofit leader, you will find plenty of people passionate about your cause and no shortage of ideas about how to better achieve it. No organization can work on everything all at once. Because nonprofits typically tend to be less well-resourced than for-profits, the strategic plan serves as the prioritizing document for how management and staff use their time.

Nonprofits are some of the most optimistic organizations in the world. People join the board and staff because they believe they can help change the world. They can, *but* there is a need for a healthy dose of practicality overlaying that optimism. While every idea may be good, not every idea is feasible. Every organization has more projects and ideas than sufficient staffing. Therefore, you need high standards for what makes it into the plan. The road to success for any organization is lined with rejected ideas, terminated pet projects, and slaughtered sacred cows.

A Strategic Plan Must Have Explicit Revenue and Financial Data

Some organizations try to exclude fundraisers from the strategic planning process. Their justification is that fundraisers will "sandbag" their goals with revenue targets they know they can achieve. Others leave the fundraisers out of the process because they view the strategic planning process as the reserve of top-tier leaders only. This is always a mistake. It is also bad management.

Effective planning and budgeting processes always consider both revenue and costs. An organization cannot manage just one side of the balance sheet. We find that many nonprofits have a detailed understanding of their costs and yet little knowledge or understanding of where their revenue comes from or why. One would not run their personal finances that way, and yet nonprofits do so all the time.

As a rule of thumb, an organization should always aspire to grow and improve. Its assumptions about what growth is possible must be based on reasonable projections. In terms of revenue growth, targets must be realistic and achievable. More importantly, the organization must have a plan for where the revenue is going to come from. Savvy nonprofits don't need to chase dollars. Instead, they attract dollars by having a solid plan and a good story to tell. Donors want to be part of a success story.

A Field Guide to Building a Strategic Plan

There are whole books on building a strategic plan, and many consultants specialize in the process. (Including the authors!) We are not big fans of cumbersome strategic planning processes or planning documents that require three-ring binders. We have found that our clients can typically step through a strategic planning process in a few weeks if they do their homework. We also believe that the best strategic plans can be explained on the front and back of a single sheet of paper.

We recommend that organizations conduct a strategic planning process every three years. Before launching the process, the board and staff must first review the current strategic plan and score themselves on how they did. Did they meet or exceed the goals they set for themselves? If so, what do they believe were the key enablers of that success? If they did not meet some of the goals they set for themselves, what were the barriers or issues that prevented them from doing so? Once the board and staff have reviewed this information and agreed upon what happened, they are ready to start a new plan.

Assemble the Strategic Planning Team

Not every board member and staff member should be invited to join the strategic planning team. Instead, there should be representative team members for the organization's various constituent groups. These representatives act as ambassadors and are tasked with taking ideas and issues to their constituencies, gathering feedback and insights, and providing that information to the team. Typically, the constituencies represented are:

- ◆ The board of directors;

- ◆ The employees of the organization, especially finance, fundraising, and program staff;

- ◆ The non-board donor community; and

- ◆ One or more individuals representing the constituency the organization serves, such as patients, students, or patrons.

The executive director or CEO *always* participates on the strategic planning team. If the position is currently vacant, the board should strongly consider waiting until a new leader has been chosen before engaging in a strategic planning process.

We find that ten to twelve members is the right size for a strategic planning team. Consider using video conference services like WebEx and Zoom. This has been a boon to the work of strategic planning consultants. Participants have fewer excuses to be late to a video conference, and the tools make it more difficult for members to distract, dominate, or redirect the team's work.

Lastly, we believe an independent strategic planning facilitator is critical to the success of the strategic planning process. A good facilitator will keep the team on track, but they can also ask critical questions and challenge assumptions because that is their role.

Key Components of the Strategic Plan

Upfront, it is essential to be clear who the key players are in a strategic plan. We believe every organization should be able to identify:

◆ The key employees;

◆ The key customers or constituents they serve; and

◆ The key stakeholders who are vested in the organization's success.

This is sometimes not a comfortable conversation for the organization to have, especially about which positions are more critical to the mission. However, not every employee has a vital role in the organization's success, and it is important to be clear about which ones must buy into the strategic plan. Ideally, the employees deemed critical to the mission are participating on the strategic planning team.

The second major component of a strategic plan is the definition of the organization's purpose and strategy. When we work with our clients to develop a strategic plan, we break this into four broad categories:

◆ The organization's defined purpose including its mission, vision, values, and brand promise;

◆ The definition of what the organization does, including its purpose, strategies, key measures of success, and "dream big" ideas;

◆ The organization's focus for the next three to five years, including a narrative of what it's going to do, how it's going to do it, and its financial and operational goals and metrics; and

◆ Specific goals, objectives, and targets for what the organization will do in the coming year.

Strategic Planning Framework

Phase 1: Current State Assessment

Phase 2: Strategy Development

Phase 3: Translate Into Work Plans

Measure & Manage Performance

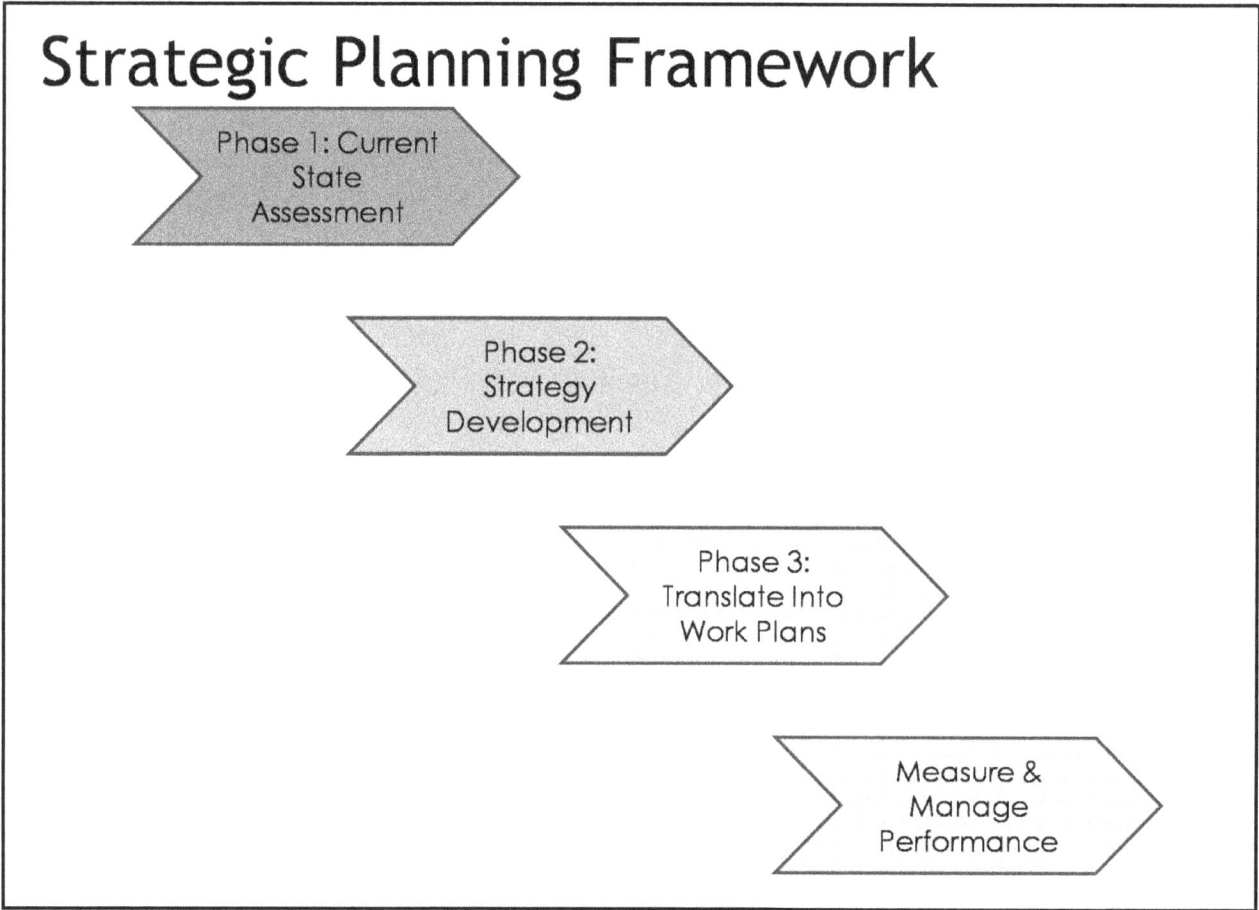

The third component of the plan provides everyone with the appropriate level of detail to understand how the organization is run. This includes the mission outcome metrics; the mission-critical processes and their metrics; critical decisions that need to be made; core competencies; the biggest barriers to success; and, the plans for overcoming those barriers.

The Process for Creating a Plan

We view strategic planning as an ongoing process, not an isolated event. The best strategic plan becomes a living document that the board and management use to run the organization and measure and report its performance.

In the first phase of planning, the organization needs to assess its current state. If there was a previous strategic plan, the team should review it again and evaluate the organization's progress against it. Did you achieve your goals? If so, how? And if you did not, what kept you from achieving them?

In this phase, the organization should also make a clear, objective scan of its environment. Who are your competitors? How are they performing against you? How do they do things? What are the barriers to entry? At this time, we find that an organization is best served by assessing its Strengths, Weaknesses, Opportunities, and Threats (known as a "SWOT") and performing a Porter's Five Forces Analysis. The latter, developed by Michael E. Porter, PhD in 1979, is a model that identifies and analyzes five competitive forces that shape every industry and helps determine that industry's weaknesses and strengths. It can be applied to any segment of the economy to understand competition within the industry and enhance its overall financial performance.

The second phase of strategic planning involves translating the lessons learned during the first phase into action plans, setting goals, and determining what is and is not feasible. In this phase, you want to be clear and concise in defining what success looks like for the organization. When you set a goal for an organization, you must always define how you will measure your performance against that goal. Good goals are "S.M.A.R.T.": Specific, Measurable, Actionable, Realistic, and Timed.

> ### Understand What Nonprofit Means!
>
> Many nonprofit leaders and boards fail to understand that "nonprofit" is a tax status. It is not a license to lose money. Your organization must still produce more than it consumes.
>
> Many tools used by for-profit companies can be useful for nonprofits but seldom are applied.

Setting a goal that says, "We will be successful at fundraising" does not meet this standard. Setting a goal that says, "Over the next three years, we will grow our annual fund by 3 percent on average yearly through improved donor cultivation and implementing a consistent solicitation schedule" does.

- "We will grow our annual fund by 3 percent on average yearly" is Specific.

- "by 3 percent on average yearly" is Measurable.

- "through improved donor cultivation and implementing a consistent solicitation schedule" is Actionable.

- "3 percent on average yearly" is Realistic.

- "over the next three years" is Timed.

In the third phase of the strategic plan, the goals you developed are translated into work plans. You will "cascade" these goals down to departments and functions throughout your organization. The fundraising goals are translated into work plans and initiatives for the development department; the mission goals are translated into work plans and initiatives for the programmatic departments; and so forth.

Once the plan is "locked," typically the board of directors votes to accept it. From that point on, for the next three years, it is an implicit requirement that management reports its progress against the goals and metrics defined by the board of directors.

Strategic Planning: The Steps

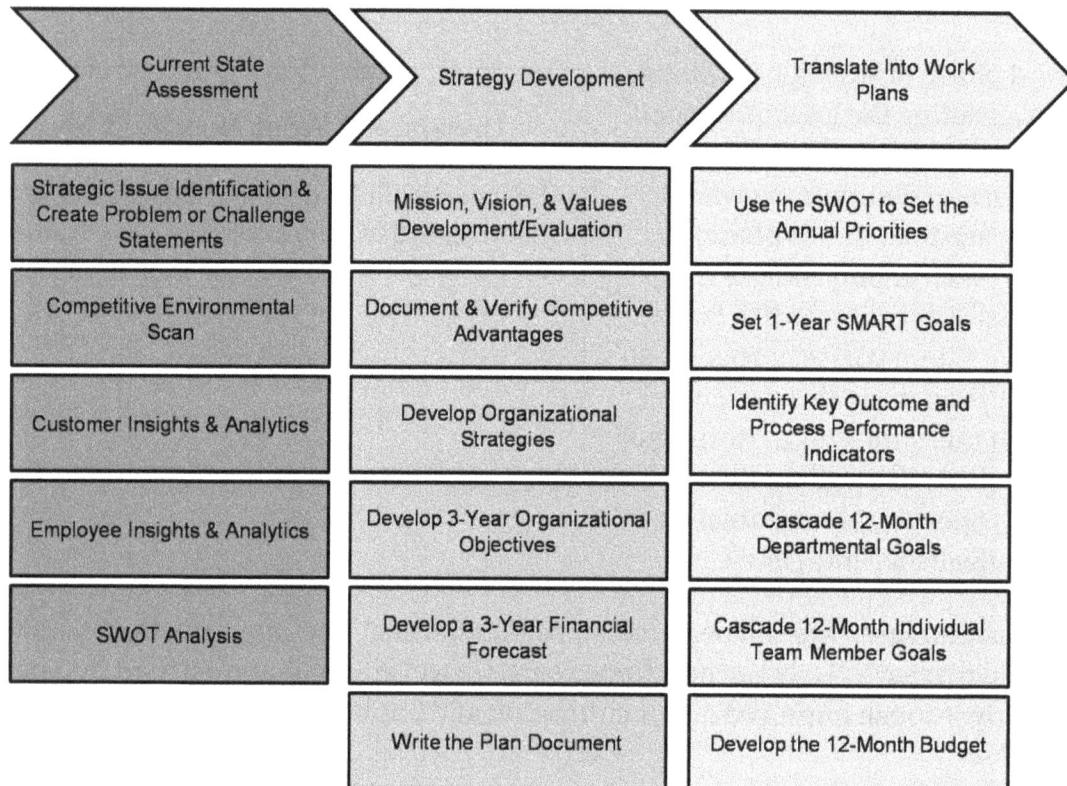

Current State Assessment	Strategy Development	Translate Into Work Plans
Strategic Issue Identification & Create Problem or Challenge Statements	Mission, Vision, & Values Development/Evaluation	Use the SWOT to Set the Annual Priorities
Competitive Environmental Scan	Document & Verify Competitive Advantages	Set 1-Year SMART Goals
Customer Insights & Analytics	Develop Organizational Strategies	Identify Key Outcome and Process Performance Indicators
Employee Insights & Analytics	Develop 3-Year Organizational Objectives	Cascade 12-Month Departmental Goals
SWOT Analysis	Develop a 3-Year Financial Forecast	Cascade 12-Month Individual Team Member Goals
	Write the Plan Document	Develop the 12-Month Budget

Suggested Ground Rules for the Process

Typically, the entire process will take eight to twelve weeks. We find that two-hour meetings every two weeks to review work done by breakout teams work best in the interim.

We believe establishing a few ground rules makes the process much more effective. First, set an expectation that *clarity of language* is critical to effective planning. Everyone's input is valuable, and project team members should leave nothing important unsaid. To ensure everyone is clear on intention, we also emphasize that candor is valued. We even go so far as to ask all the team members to promise to not be offended by anything said in the meeting room.

For the CEO or executive director and the board chair, we ask them to explicitly commit to the team that there are *no political landmines* in the process. Nothing is or should be personal.

Second, we advise teams to *avoid philosophical mineshafts*. The strategic planning process should stick to the realm of reasonable assumptions, opportunities, and initiatives. Many people will want to take a "white paper" approach, meaning starting with a blank page and reimagining everything about the organization. While this can be a fun exercise in imagination, it seldom changes the outcome of the plan. Mostly, it is just a waste of time.

Third, set the expectation that team members should *respect the sanctity of the team meetings.* The team meetings are for building agreement, establishing understanding and consensus. Team members should show up with their homework done and should not manage projects in the team meeting.

Lastly, because one of the challenges of nonprofit board service is for management and board members to stay in their respective lanes, the team should always attempt to *be clear on matters of "governance" versus "management."* The board does not own management's duties, and management cannot usurp the board's governance role.

To Recap

◆ The strategic plan and fundraising plan are closely related. Many funders expect you to produce the strategic plan and show how you measure progress against it.

◆ Every nonprofit organization needs a strategic plan. It becomes both a road map and a report card for how the organization is performing.

◆ The process does not need to be complicated. The best strategic plans are only a few pages long.

Chapter Two

The Role of the Chief Development Officer

IN THIS CHAPTER

···→ There are definable characteristics of an effective development office.

···→ The role and responsibilities of the development officer are complex and should be understood and supported by the executive director.

···→ Budgeting, databases, moves management, and stewardship...oh my!

Development is the process of building long-term, positive, and mutually beneficial relationships between donors and the nonprofit. The role of the development office is to identify prospects; educate them about the organization's mission; relate how a fundraising campaign affects prospects and their families; involve the prospects by eliciting their opinions and support; secure investment from prospects; and steward the donor relationship to ensure repeat gifts.

> **Fundraising Is a Team Sport**
>
> The executive director, the development staff, and the board of directors share fundraising responsibility.

The development responsibility is shared by the executive director, the board, other volunteers, and the development staff.

Size and Structure of a Development Office

Let's start with the elephant in the room. Many boards of directors question the expense of fundraisers. We frequently get the question, "How many fundraisers do we really need?" The answer is, of course, "that depends."

In 2018, the Chicago-based Pierce Family Foundation conducted a survey of nonprofits to determine how many full-time equivalent (FTE) fundraisers were needed to raise $1 million. They found that the average answer was two. Basically, for every $500,000 an organization needs to raise, one FTE must be dedicated to fundraising on average. While this is a useful soundbite to use with boards, the real answer is much more complex. Where the organization is in its life cycle, the momentum that already exists in fundraising, and the ability of the organization to invest all impact the actual number. If an organization has never had a full-time fundraiser or a formalized fundraising program, it would be unreasonable to hire a fundraiser and immediately expect them to produce $500,000 in their first year.

While the size of the development team may vary, most nonprofits do have at least one staff member whose primary responsibility is fundraising. The primary duties of the development officer include annual fundraising, major and capital fundraising, planned giving, donor research, donor records maintenance, corporate and foundation research, donor communications, and donor relations. The size of the staff will depend upon the size of the nonprofit, how long the development office has been in place, and the organization's fundraising goals.

An effective development office includes:

- An experienced chief development officer using best fundraising practices;

- An effective partnership between the development officer and the Executive Director;

- Good working relationships between the development officer and the board of directors and development committee members;

- Well-trained support staff and volunteers;

- A well-articulated case for support grounded in the strategic plan;

- A comprehensive annual development plan as well as three- to five-year goals based on the strategic plan;

- Strong fundraising policies and procedures;

- A sound donor management system; and,

- A strong cultivation and stewardship program.

The titles "Director of Development (DoD)" and "Chief Development Officer (CDO)" are generalist titles and are used to describe the leader of the development office functions. This role can encompass all major gift fundraising and campaign management in addition to annual fundraising responsibilities and overall management of the development staff. It is not unusual for a nonprofit of any size to have a DoD/CDO, an annual fund manager, an events manager, and administrative support. Larger nonprofits may have additional staff members who focus on major gifts, planned giving, donor research, and database management.

Ideal Qualifications of a Director of Development

It is typically preferred for a director of development to have earned, at a minimum, a bachelor's degree. Successful candidates have a minimum of three to five years of successful managerial/leadership experience in fundraising or applicable roles (e.g., marketing, sales, or revenue management) with progressive growth of responsibilities. The DoD will have a demonstrated track record of applicable achievements in:

◆ Innovative strategizing for the growth of new revenue opportunities;

◆ Personal solicitations of high-net-worth individuals;

◆ Face-to-face donor meetings and relationship building; and

◆ Achieving increased revenue goals.

Development officers must have outstanding written and verbal communication skills, extraordinary interpersonal skills, business etiquette, and attention to detail. They must be team players with the ability to both lead and follow. This role will need to operate in concert with all departments within the organization, particularly the public relations/marketing and finance departments, and should possess the ability to collaborate effectively.

Knowledge of a sound donor management system/donor records/research system and using data mining and predictive modeling is advantageous for the development officer to facilitate giving.

It will be the responsibility of the development officer to maintain an effective stewardship program for donors, including acknowledgment, recognition, and engagement.

The Role and Responsibilities of the Development Officer

It is essential for the executive director and the organization's leadership to fully understand the director of development's expansive responsibilities and support all fundraising efforts. This is a challenging and complex job. The development profession historically has had a high rate of turnover. Hiring the most qualified professional that the organization can afford is a great start, but the development officer must be treated well to achieve longevity. A leadership team that understands its workload and shows appreciation goes a long way. The longer development officers are in place, the better the job they will do. Fundraising is all about relationships; therefore, the longevity of the development officer breeds better long-term fundraising results for the organization.

Director of Development Job Description

Summary:

The Director of Development (DoD) supports the Executive Director and nonprofit leadership to achieve the organization's fundraising goals. This position plays a vital role in ensuring the long-term financial health and viability of the organization.

The Director of Development manages the process of building long-term, positive, and mutually beneficial relationships between donors and the nonprofit to fund the organization's operational and capital needs based on the strategic plan.

Primary Responsibilities:

- Manages the development team of staff and volunteers and collaborates to secure gifts from individual donors, corporations, foundations, and other organizations.

- Develops strategies for achieving fundraising goals.

- Meets with donors and prospects to create and foster relationships and create a balanced funding mix of donor sources and solicitation programs tailored to the organization's needs.

- Responsible for the cultivation, solicitation, and acknowledgment of donations, including the creation of proposals and applications; ensuring the reporting, forecasting, and accuracy of donor records; and creating or approving messaging regarding the organization and its fundraising programs.

- Works collaboratively with the organization's leaders and volunteers and is charged with prospecting for new donors or opportunities to increase donations from existing donors.

- Manages the activities of the development committee. Board members and development committee members are expected to participate in, organize, and support key activities, including but not limited to volunteer events, promotions, and cultivation activities.

- Maintains and reports performance metrics toward goals and performs other duties and responsibilities assigned by the executive director.

- Crafts written requests that secure support from individuals, foundations, and corporations.

- Ensures that all requests and/or proposals address all identified requirements and represent the organization in a clear, professional, and brand-appropriate manner. The DoD may be required to conduct financial and/or marketing analysis to support the creation of the proposal and is expected to ensure the accuracy and clarity of all data and findings.

- Ensures that all solicitations are completed, reviewed, approved, and submitted in advance of deadlines.

The Donor Lifecycle

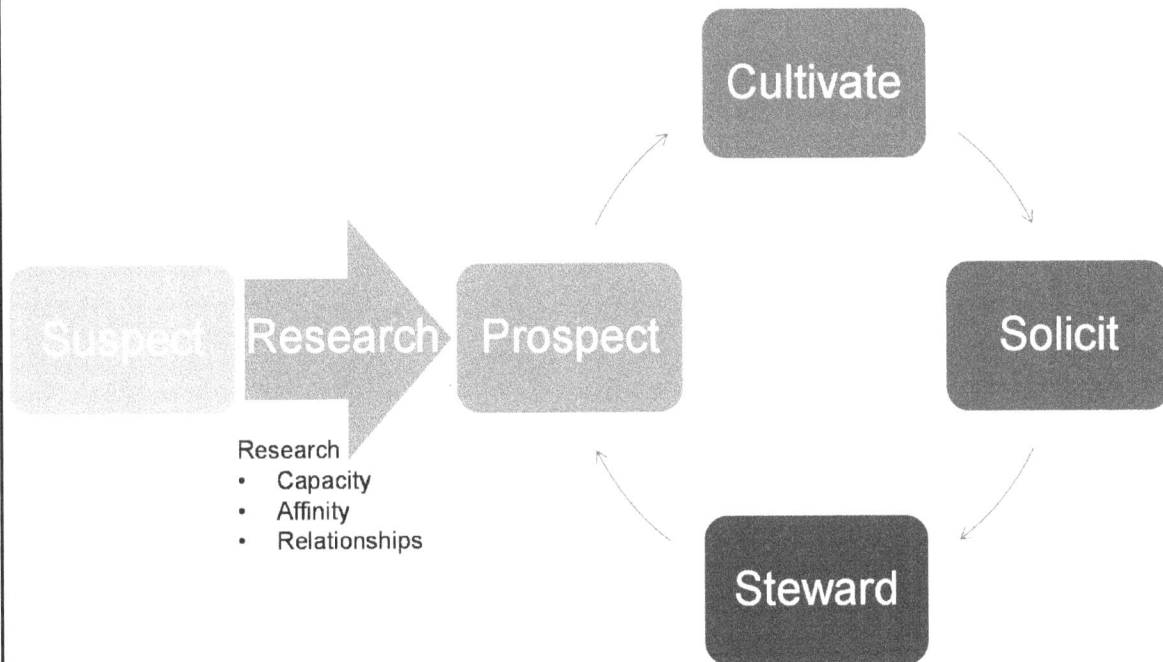

Suspect **Research** Prospect

Research
- Capacity
- Affinity
- Relationships

Cultivate

Solicit

Steward

The DoD Identifies and Evaluates New Funding Sources

Since funding strategies vary over time, the director of development must continually work to evaluate potential matches with the organization's goals. The DoD is expected to use research tools and other available resources (including the board of directors) to identify donors whose interests align with the organization's mission and represent a funding opportunity.

Prospect research identifies and evaluates prospective donors, whether they are individuals, businesses, or foundations. This research reveals background information on a donor or prospect that determines what type of cultivation and solicitation should occur. It is useful in preparing for annual fund drives and is critical in advancing a capital campaign. Organizations often shortchange this process and therefore do not achieve maximum results.

Donor/prospect research is not a one-time event, which means the development office should have an established process for continual prospect research. If you do not have a development staff member dedicated to research, the task can be assigned to a summer intern or another employee's administrative task.

Begin research with past and current donor lists. Do not just look at the top donors but also give special attention to those who have given consistently over time. Online sources can also help you determine what individuals might share your organization's vision. *Suspects—* individuals who are not yet prospects—can be contacted and congratulated about whatever is newsworthy. You can also share something with them about your organization, thereby turning suspects into prospects.

In researching your top prospects, no detail is too small. You never know when you can make a connection between a donor or prospect's interest and something going on at your nonprofit. This information can be gathered from the news, from your colleagues, or from volunteers. Some prospects will even tell you things about themselves that might be useful in a future solicitation. Useful donor/prospect information to collect includes:

- name;

- address(es);

- telephone number(s);

- business-related information including title, address, and phone;

- marital status;

- names, number, and ages of children;

- date and place of birth;

- education;

- spouse/partner information;

- connections to the nonprofit;

- job history;

- honors and achievements;

- clubs and organizations;

- political affiliations;

- religious affiliations;

- personal interests;

- estimated net worth;

◆ directorships;

◆ family foundations;

◆ favorite charities;

◆ charitable giving record;

◆ name(s) of assistant(s);

◆ attorney, accountant, and/or banker;

◆ close friends; and,

◆ other relatives who have a relationship with the organization.

Sources of research data include telephone directories, ZIP code directories, Who's Who in America; social registers; Standard & Poor's Register of Corporate Executives and Directors; Dun & Bradstreet's Million Dollar Directory; local newspapers and news of organizations similar to yours in the community; directories and memberships of local clubs and organizations; property rolls; influential contacts and volunteers; and other online computer sources.

For corporate research, identify the full name of the contact persons and their correct addresses; corporate assets; type of business; list of corporate officers and directors; list of directors if a corporate foundation; sales volume; previous giving record; the decision-making process; gifts to nonprofits; connections to your nonprofit (if any); if a national company, local subsidiaries and officers; corporate gift committee, connections, and historical interests; and corporate annual report.

Foundation research will include the full and correct name of the foundation; correct address and phone number; names of directors and their professional connections; historical information including when founded, by whom and for what purpose; current assets; history of recent grants; the decision-making process; foundation contact to visit; details on where and how to submit a proposal; connections to the nonprofit; recent IRS 990; most recent annual report; deadlines for proposals; dates of board meetings; the average size of grants; and other instructions.

Electronic wealth screenings are additional tools that provide a meaningful way of culling massive lists into a smaller, more manageable list of prospects. It is fast, painless, and relatively inexpensive. Many companies offer services that will compare your records to a multitude of sources and provide enough information so that you can target your top prospects for annual and major giving. They do not usually provide new names; they tell you about the names on your list. These wealth screenings can be helpful, but they do not provide any assessment of an individual's inclination to give to your organization. However, these data mining services can help set appropriate campaign goals by analyzing your entire database to identify your best annual, major, and planned giving prospects.

Executive Directors must be aware of the importance of research to the development operation. Once prospects have been identified, a defined and strategic cultivation plan should be developed for each prospect with an identified timing and solicitation goal. Additionally, you will need a system to manage the data and make assignments to your staff and volunteers.

The DoD Maintains Database of Accurate and Confidential Donor Information

The development office must maintain an accurate and pertinent database that includes all current and previous donors and prospects. Much of the background information included will be gleaned during the research process. All touchpoints with a donor/prospect should be tracked in the database, including phone calls, cultivation and stewardship activities, solicitations by method and rate of return, pledges, pledge reminders, and acknowledgments. The database should provide easily accessible reporting tools. This database should be kept highly confidential, and only those with a need to know should be given access.

The DoD Creates and Manages the Annual Development Plan

Every year, the DoD should create and submit a comprehensive development plan with annual objectives that are rooted in the organization's strategic goals. This plan should be presented to the executive director and the development committee for approval and implementation. The development officer cannot and should not be expected to do all the fundraising. It is a group effort with the executive director assuming a leadership role. Refer to Chapter Three for details on annual development planning.

The DoD Produces and Oversees the Development Office Budget

The budgetary process for the development office begins with the development officer, in conjunction with the executive director, identifying the fundraising goals necessary to meet the nonprofit's current and future strategic goals. Fundraising goals should be realistic and based on data of both the organization's need and the community's capacity to give. With this knowledge, the development officer determines the financial resources necessary to meet those goals.

Donors Care About Fundraising Expenses

As a rule of thumb, fundraising expenses should never exceed 25 percent. Said plainly, for every one dollar raised, donors expect you to spend less than twenty-five cents to raise it.

The budget of the development office should include both staff salaries and fundraising resources. In a well-run annual fund, the total cost per dollar raised is less than twenty-five cents. Capital campaigns are even more efficient: the cost may be in the 5 to 7 percent range. As a nonprofit leader, remember that it takes money to raise money. There must be an infusion of resources to increase the total amount of money raised.

The DoD Spends a Great Deal of Time Out of the Office

Development officers should be out of the office much of the time. In addition to soliciting gifts, this time should be spent engaging in the cultivation and stewardship of volunteers and prospects. If the development staff is tied to the office because of administrative duties, explore other ways to accommodate these tasks.

> ### Get Out of the Office
>
> Development officers should be out of the office as much as, or more than, they are in the office. As fundraising goals increase, or during campaign seasons, it may be necessary to increase the development staff's size to eliminate barriers that would otherwise hinder the ability to get out of the office.

There is no specific number of calls or solicitations required of the development officer in any given month. However, visits must be planned, or it is easy to get so busy behind the desk that time slips away with no personal calls being made.

Tips for scheduling visits:

◆ Block off one hour per week to schedule visits with donors and prospects for the next week or two.

◆ Similarly, block off one consistent day each week to be out of the office. Plan to schedule three to five calls (visits) depending upon where the donors/prospects are located. While meetings should occur when it is most convenient for the donor/prospect, keeping your schedule as consistent as possible will help eliminate other distractions popping up on those days.

◆ Schedule coffee or breakfast meetings every morning on the way into the office.

Development work often falls outside of the standard nine-to-five workday. In staffing the development operation, consider that, in addition to office responsibilities, coverage of events and meetings will require more labor than other departments.

With the executive director's support, the development officer should evaluate development staffing to ensure adequate coverage of all development tasks while also giving the chief development officer the ability to be out of the office regularly. Are more staff members needed, or can tasks be reassigned? Will a new staff position pay for itself in increased productivity and results? Can volunteers assist with administrative overflow? Is there a need for additional technology or equipment? Can outside services or consultants help?

The DoD Supervises Staff and Volunteers

The development director may have oversight responsibility for development staff, grant writers, consultants, contractors, and volunteers. The DoD is responsible for ensuring that contributed revenue goals are met or exceeded annually in each giving area. The DoD strategizes with leadership on creating and implementing annual work plans for staff and ensures work plans/goals are on target. The DoD provides leadership, mentoring, and training to the development team members and fosters an environment of successful teamwork and cross-assignment collaboration.

> ### Warning! Know Your Lane!
>
> The development committee is an integral part of the development operation. It works at the discretion of, and in collaboration with, the development officer and executive director but never as a separate entity.

In addition to staff, the DoD is responsible for the supervision and compliance of fundraising volunteers, including but not limited to board members and the development committee. The development committee is an integral part of the development operation. It works at the discretion of, and in collaboration with, the development officer and executive director but never as a separate entity.

The DoD Ensures Compliance with All Reporting Requirements

The DoD is responsible for the reporting process and ensures compliance with all requirements. Donors, particularly foundations, may have annual reporting requirements for detailing how their support was put to use. The finance department typically handles end-of-year donation statements, but the development office is responsible for the accurate reporting of giving. The development office is also responsible for creating and distributing the annual report, an overview of the nonprofit's financials. It typically includes a list of donors by campaign or giving level.

The DoD Manages the Moves Management Process

Moves management is a nonprofit term for the process of donor development. After identifying and qualifying a prospect, it is literally the process of *moving* that prospect through cultivation to the solicitation. The moves management process should be managed by the development office and tracked either in the database or, in small organizations without a database, on a spreadsheet.

Moves require action steps. Once identified and qualified, each donor/prospect is assigned to a solicitor—staff, leadership, board, development committee members, or other volunteers. Each solicitor makes cultivation and solicitation requests and reports progress to the development office. These activities must be carefully coordinated, especially if the prospect is assigned to more than one solicitor. The lead solicitor drives the moves management for the prospect.

The development officer will set up the overall prospect strategy and status and then add new actions. To ensure a comprehensive record of each prospect, the database should summarize each action taken to date with that prospect.

The order of priority for setting up prospect action records is:

- Top campaign prospects;

- Top annual giving prospects that are not campaign prospects; and

- Board members and other VIP donors not in another prospect category.

The prospect strategy and status should summarize the intended strategy or outcome in one sentence, set the projected ask amount, and define the classification status. Include each prospect in up to five cultivation activities over a three- to six-month period. The next stages are solicitation and then closing.

In moves management, the development officer must closely monitor open records and ensure that they remain accurate and updated. All open actions with deadlines pending within the week should be reviewed weekly with each solicitor. Actions that are overdue for more than a week are given a red flag and should be discussed in a bi-monthly meeting.

Solicitors should complete call reports on each and every visit. Each call report should end with one or more subsequent steps. For each prospect, be sure to set a next significant move, such as scheduling a facilities tour or setting a lunch next month to make the ask.

A summary of moves management information should be shared in an "action items" report and regularly reviewed at development committee meetings or with other non-committee volunteers and staff.

Database updates can be verbal downloads from the solicitor, either by dictation, in person, via telephone, or via voicemail. Updates can be via emails. They can be formal written reports. They can be notes scribbled on the margin of a document. What is essential is that they be timely and relevant to moving the prospect forward. Contact reports should be in the database within twenty-four to forty-eight hours of the contact, simultaneously generated with a thank-you note or follow-up correspondence.

It is a good practice to store all briefing notes, directions, and prospect preferences (e.g., doesn't like breakfast meetings, doesn't drive after dark) in database notes, as well. This makes it easy to prepare for subsequent visits.

Practical Tip

Solicitors should complete call reports on each and every prospect visit within twenty-four to forty-eight hours of the contact. These reports can either be directly recorded in the database or submitted to the development administrative staff to input on the solicitor's behalf.

After a gift or pledge has been made, the donor is assigned to a stewardship strategy. On the other hand, if the request is denied but the donor indicates a willingness to be reapproached, the prospect returns to cultivation. If the request is rejected and the prospect has no interest, then this prospect should be coded as "no longer a prospect."

The DoD Oversees the Donor Stewardship Strategy

Donor stewardship is perhaps the most crucial part of the donor relationship. Unfortunately, it is also the portion of the relationship many nonprofits most frequently neglect. The development department is often so overwhelmed by other duties that stewardship seems like the area that can be skimped. Meeting a donor for coffee or lunch just to catch up can seem like a luxury for which they may not have time. However, this cannot be further from the truth.

As stated before, development is the process of building long-term, positive, and mutually beneficial relationships between donors and the nonprofit. If that's true, it means that what happens after the gift is secured is just as important, or perhaps more, to continuing that relationship. If your donors feel that they only hear from you when the organization needs money (e.g., "it's time for the annual fund again!"), then they may feel that you view them as an ATM instead of as a friend of the organization.

Tips for an effective and implementable stewardship plan include the following:

◆ Create a plan. (You've got to start somewhere!) On an easy-to-view spreadsheet, list the names of all major donors and one individualized stewardship touchpoint (not an ask) to be completed each month. Keep this on your desktop and review regularly.

◆ Say "Thank You!" regularly and in different ways. The gift acknowledgment letter sent immediately after a gift or pledge is received is expected (and required!) Subsequent shows of appreciation are received more genuinely. Have a board member or client call to say thank you; send a handwritten note; say "thank you" again each time you see the donor.

◆ Treat major donors like VIPs. Send a personal email with an organizational update or accomplishment before it's announced in the next newsletter. If opening a new building or instituting a new program, provide major donors with the chance to be the first to view it. Ask their opinion on something.

◆ Personally invite major donors to join you at a program, sit with you at an event, or tour the facilities. Group activities decrease the time commitment, but the more one-on-one interactions you can pull off, the better.

◆ Schedule at least one non-solicitation one-on-one meeting each year. Coffees and lunches are the easiest to secure but look for other creative ways to engage with major donors as well. When Ailena worked at a healthcare nonprofit, leaders of a large corporate sponsor were also personal donors. Each Christmas, this company fielded a team of employees to volunteer at a local toy drive. Ailena, along with other staff members, volunteered alongside them for many years. While doing good for the community, they could also forge meaningful relationships with these individuals through this shared experience.

◆ Do what you say you'll do. Trust is the basis of all effective relationships, and that includes donor relationships. So it goes without saying that the organization should go to great lengths to ensure that trust is upheld. If something changes, such as the funding priorities, go back to the donor and explain. Most of the time, donors understand. What they won't understand is why they may have heard of it from other donors or in the news rather than from you.

To Recap

◆ Fundraising responsibility is shared by the executive director, the development staff, and the board of trustees.

◆ The executive director and organization leaders need to understand and appreciate the tasks assigned to the development officer. Acknowledgment, support, and appreciation of the development officer can positively affect tenure and thereby increase fundraising effectiveness.

◆ Donor stewardship is just as important as all other development responsibilities.

Chapter Three

Three Secrets to Successful Fundraising

IN THIS CHAPTER

- ···→ Talking about your organization and its fundraising plans

- ···→ Fundraising leadership goes beyond staff

- ···→ Planning for Success (Spoiler: You have to write it down!)

What are these three secrets that will bring radical organizational change and set you up for success? Turns out, they're not so secret...or radical. However, they are fundamentally vital to your efforts and the starting point for every successful fundraising enterprise. No matter the organization, solicitor, or campaign, successful fundraising boils down to three key elements: a compelling case, committed leadership, and a written action plan. Of everything you stand to learn through this book, this section may be the most important. (So take notes!)

Before starting each fiscal year, schedule a significant amount of time to devote yourself and your team to planning. Pull out this chapter and review it together. It might help to schedule this planning session at an off-site location. A comfortable space with no distractions helps speed the process along while offering an atmosphere to be creative in considering each element fresh each year.

A Compelling Case for Support

Why should a donor contribute to your organization? Why this campaign specifically? What differentiates your organization from another? What is the compelling reason a donor should pull out a credit card or checkbook and support your cause?

Together, your team should spend time answering these questions in detail. Once agreed upon and vetted by leadership, the culmination should be the "elevator speech" and the written case for support.

The Elevator Speech

Imagine you run into a "friend" of the organization at the coffee shop who asks you about the latest campaign. In thirty seconds or less, can you summarize the organization's current fundraising campaign in a compelling way that makes the prospect want to know more? Furthermore, can the board, organization's leadership, and key volunteers do the same?

Start with answering these questions for each campaign:

◆ What do you need funds for?

◆ Why is it important?

◆ Why should someone financially support it?

Craft the answers to these questions into a persuasive "elevator speech" that you can give spur of the moment. Your board and other leaders need to have these same talking points. Spend time as a group role-playing to ensure everyone is on the same page. While everyone can, and should, make the talking points their own, practicing will ensure they understand and cover the crucial elements. Everyone involved in fundraising, and even those in leadership positions who are not directly in fundraising, should be able to discuss fundraising efforts in a succinct and unified manner.

This short, concise description forms the basis of all other funding efforts, including the written case for support, solicitation letters, foundation proposals, and marketing materials.

The Written Case for Support

The support case refers to the written document providing a prospect with details about the campaign and information needed to make an informed gift decision. A case for support for the annual fund or an endowment campaign may only be one page and sometimes in the form of a promotional flyer, while the case for support for a capital campaign is typically in the range of three to five pages. While some organizations' cases can be longer due to their choice of graphics and layout, three to five pages are plenty to adequately cover the topic in detail and ensure you don't lose your reader's attention. This document is graphically designed to be both printed and in a digital format. It is used as a leave-behind document—never as a standalone solicitation piece—after an in-person solicitation for prospects to refer to when making their gift decisions.

Know your audience and culture. While some organization's prospect pool might be wooed by an expensively printed case for support with ten pages of glossy graphics, another organization's constituents might look at that same document as a misuse of funds and respond better to a simply designed piece printed in-house. Once, at a fundraising dinner for top donors, Ailena had a well-respected major donor beeline her way across the ballroom at the close of the presentation. Waving the multi-page, high gloss donor packet, she asked, "I know how much it costs to print something like this. Is this what you spent my money on? Because if it is, I'm not giving you any more!" Luckily, Ailena could reply that the printing for the event was generously covered through an in-kind gift from one of the sponsors. However, that was a lesson she never forgot.

The support case should include:

    ◆ A brief history of your organization written specifically to inform the reader of where the organization has come from and culminating in how the organization got to where you are today;

    ◆ A detailed overview of the campaign, including fundraising goals, details of the projects to be completed through the campaign, and the overall budget; and

    ◆ A "frequently asked questions" section to answer common questions, including how to make a gift.

Remember, this piece should be compelling. Go beyond just stating the details. Tell a story from the cover page through the end. If your campaign has a theme, it should be woven throughout the document. Use pictures to tell the story and include any images or renderings available to highlight the intended projects.

When assembling the packet for your in-person major gift solicitations, the support case should be accompanied by a pledge form and a personalized one-page "ask" letter signed by leadership summarizing the campaign discussed and including the specific donation request made during the meeting.

The Solicitation Meeting Packet

After each in-person solicitation of a major gift prospect, you should leave behind a meeting packet that includes the case for support, a pledge form, and a personalized ask letter that includes a specific donation request. Make it as easy as possible for the prospect to make a commitment by auto-filling the pledge form with name and contact information.

What if the amount you were planning to ask for changes during the meeting? Simply remove the ask letter before leaving the packet, then email the letter in your follow-up within twenty-four hours.

Committed Leadership

Of the three secrets to fundraising success, leadership may be the most critical. You can have a mediocre case for support and still raise money when led by a trusted, charismatic leader. However, this should not be an excuse to ignore the other two secrets to success! "Leadership" in this context refers to both staff and volunteers who can come from a variety of constituency groups. Fundraising is always a team effort. No one person, even the best fundraiser among us, can do it alone. Instead of a "one size fits all" approach to solicitation using the same one or two individuals, ask, "Who is most likely to receive a yes from this prospect?" A separate solicitation plan should be created for each prospect, including choosing a solicitor to whom the prospect would most likely say yes.

Committed leadership includes:

> **Fundraising Myth**
>
> "It's the staff's job to raise money." We've heard this a lot from inexperienced executive directors and board members. Not only is it physically impossible for one or two staff members to personally solicit every prospective major donor (on top of their other duties), but also nonsensical to think they would be the individual best received by every single prospect. Instead, ask the question, "Who is most likely to get a yes from this prospect?"

◆ The Executive Director—The "ED" participates as an engaged and active solicitor who may be directly or indirectly involved in campaign planning. During a campaign, roughly 50 percent of an ED's job should include fundraising activities, including soliciting, prospect cultivation activities, and donor stewardship.

◆ Development Staff—All aspects of the organization's fundraising efforts are directed and managed by members of the development staff, including campaign direction/ management, prospecting, donor cultivation, solicitations, gift processing, gift acknowledgments, and stewardship.

◆ Board of Directors—First, it is imperative that 100 percent of your board financially supports all fundraising activities, including the annual fund, capital campaigns, and annual special events. One of the first questions a foundation will ask is the percentage of board participation in your campaign. Board participation is a show of internal support for the organization and its efforts. Nothing less than 100 percent is acceptable. Second, all boards are fundraising boards, no matter what they say! While only some may be willing to actively participate in soliciting prospects, all board members can cultivate relationships, share contacts, and show appreciation for gifts.

> **Fundraising Myth**
>
> "This isn't a fundraising board." There is no such thing! One of the main responsibilities of the board of directors is to ensure the fiscal strength and accountability of the organization. To do that, individual members must do their part to support the development efforts. This certainly might include soliciting for a gift, but might also include activities such as hosting coffees/ lunches to cultivate relationships with potential donors, making thank-you calls or handwriting thank-you notes to donors, and being an active champion of the organization and its development efforts in the community.

◆ Leadership Team—While not necessarily active solicitors, all leadership team members should feel informed and equipped to serve as champions of the campaign. Most likely, they are the face of the organization to a group of constituents that you and other campaign leaders are not, and therefore likely to be asked questions. However, don't overlook staff members as potential fundraisers just because that isn't their job. Some of the best campaign leaders and solicitors we've found have simply been staff members who were beloved and "hard to say no to!"

◆ Development Committee—A development committee is a group of volunteers committed to actively engaging and soliciting major gifts to ensure the organization successfully meets all fundraising campaign goals. The development committee is comprised of board members and sometimes rounded out by additional trusted, highly engaged volunteers. A board member who serves as the development liaison to the board most always chairs it.

◆ Annual Fund Committee—This committee focuses its efforts on the success of the annual fund. The development committee, or a member of the development committee who sits on the annual fund committee, and staff solicit major gifts for the annual fund. Refer to Chapter Seven for additional information on the annual fund committee structure.

◆ Capital Campaign Committee—This committee focuses its efforts on the success of a capital campaign. Typically, the development committee transitions to form this committee during a campaign. Additional volunteers can be added specifically for the campaign's duration and roll off once the campaign is completed. This means that a board member would typically chair the capital campaign committee. However, there are certainly instances where a non-board member became the more obvious choice due to their influence and charisma. In that case, you might consider their service as a test-run for a board nomination. Refer to Chapter Eight for additional information on capital campaign committee structure.

Good fundraising volunteers will have these attributes.

◆ The number-one quality is a willingness to participate. Anyone can solicit a gift when given the proper tools.

◆ Good volunteers should be champions of the organization.

◆ They are well respected by the organization's community.

◆ Ideally, they should be hard to say no to.

◆ They absolutely must be donors themselves.

When Ailena became the director of development at a private school, her first task was to reinstate a lapsed annual fund among a constituency that had not been solicited adequately for donations in years. She decided the most important goal for that first year, beyond even the financial goal, was to create a culture of philanthropy through strategic education. The key to this would be committed volunteer leadership. She asked staff for the name of a parent that was well respected, highly involved, and willing to jump in to help whenever asked, spoke well of the school's efforts in the community, and, most importantly, was hard to say no to.

One name immediately came to everyone's minds, and that parent was quickly recruited to serve as the campaign chair. This mother had never served in a fundraising role like this, but she was willing to learn and quickly recruited a team of equally enthusiastic volunteers. She gave the agreed-upon elevator speech to everyone who would listen; she wrote and signed ask letters; she stood in the parents' carline cheering and asked other parents to participate; she made phone calls and sent text messages. She was a true champion. And, by the end of the campaign, countless individuals walked into the development office and said, "I can't say no to her, so I'm here to donate to the annual fund. What is it again, and how much do I give?" By the third year of her involvement, the annual fund went from nonexistent to roughly 80 percent parent participation.

It doesn't take a trained, seasoned professional to raise money. Sometimes a charismatic, respected volunteer willing to carry out a portion of the development plan can get the job done even better.

The Development Plan

You must have a written fundraising plan. This plan clearly defines your fundraising goals for the fiscal year broken down by campaign and answers the "who, what, when, where, and how" for each. Start with defining the campaign's financial goal. The rest of the plan should consist of the strategies for reaching that goal broken down by constituent groups, including (but obviously not limited to) board, staff, previous board members, previous donors, and LYBUNT/

Industry Terms

LYBUNT—Donors who gave Last Year But Unfortunately Not This Year.

SYBUNT—Donors who give Some Years But Unfortunately Not This Year.

These industry terms refer to lapsed donors that either gave last year but not yet this year (LYBUNT) or have given one or more times in the past five years (SYBUNT) but not in the previous or current year to date. They are not current donors, nor are they new prospective donors. Special attention should be given to these donor groups to identify what or who motivated them to give previously, why they have not yet given, and what strategies might best work to secure a new gift.

SYBUNT (see sidebar). It must include appropriate cultivation and stewardship plans as well as a timeline for the implementation of all elements. A sample plan outline is provided at the end of this chapter.

A Wealth of Fundraising Resources

There is a wealth of fundraising opportunities and considerable resources available to help you further your fundraising knowledge.

The Association of Fundraising Professionals (AFP) is the professional association of individuals and organizations that generate philanthropic support for a wide variety of charitable institutions in chapters worldwide. It requires members to comply with a Code of Ethical Principles and Standards designed to provide concrete guidelines for fundraising professionals. AFP created the Donor Bill of Rights that outlines what donors have the right to expect from charitable organizations to which they contribute. AFP raises awareness of philanthropy by offering programs such as National Philanthropy Day, Youth programs, and philanthropist and fundraiser awards/recognition.

CFRE International is an independent nonprofit organization whose sole mission is to set standards in philanthropy through a valid and reliable certification process for fundraising professionals. In 2013, the Certified Fund Raising Executive (CFRE) credential became available worldwide as the global standard for the fundraising profession.

Giving USA: The Annual Report on Philanthropy is the seminal publication reporting on the sources and uses of charitable giving in the United States. First published in 1956, it is the longest-running, most comprehensive report on philanthropy in the United States. Its research, conducted by the Indiana University Lilly Family School of Philanthropy, estimates all giving to all charitable organizations across the United States and provides the most accurate estimates and trend data on charitable giving.

There are many other organizations beyond these. Most are unique to the specific sector in which the organization exists. Research what other organizations support your sector.

Ethics and Compliance

As you establish your fundraising plans, keep the following in mind. In many cases, it is helpful to establish written ethics and compliance guidelines and policies approved by the board so that everyone is on the same page.

- ◈ Legal landscape: Stay abreast of local, state, and federal guidelines.

- ◈ Transparency: Have an annual audit conducted by an outside auditor. Specific attention should be given to the valuation of gifts, including auction items, real estate, and stocks. Make sure donors and prospects can easily find your financials on your website and through public resources.

◆ Fundraising compliance: Be familiar with and comply with all charitable solicitation regulations in your state.

◆ Preferential treatment: Do not accept gifts that raise improper flags related to the relationship or treatment of a constituent. Gifts should not influence or even offer a perceived influence on the relationship between a donor and the nonprofit or elevate the decision-making influence on a donor.

◆ Maintain boundaries: Some major donors may want or feel they deserve more influence within the nonprofit. Maintain boundaries and a high level of professionalism at all times.

◆ Gift acceptance policies: Ensure you have a strong gift acceptance policy that outlines the type of gifts accepted and under what parameters, which donations are not accepted, and which gifts require review by a predetermined gift acceptance committee. Some gifts come

> **Watch Out!**
>
> It is hard to imagine, but sometimes you may have to turn down a gift. A gift acceptance policy clearly defines what gifts are acceptable, not acceptable, or need further review.

with too many restrictions or with negative connotations that would, in the long run, not be worth the risk to your organization. Examples include real estate or gifts connected to donors with legal or public relations issues. An agreed-upon policy gives you the authority to refuse a gift.

◆ Donor privacy: Who should be given access to donor records? Data should only be made available to those individuals who have a need to know.

◆ Volunteer management: Volunteers and their activities need to be supervised. Volunteers should be trained. Access to confidential information should be limited, and all volunteers need to know that information must remain confidential.

To Recap

◆ Successful fundraising requires a compelling case for support, committed leadership, and a written development plan.

◆ The support case is an essential element of the solicitation process, used as a leave-behind document.

◆ Leadership consists of both staff and volunteers.

◆ Behind every good campaign is a written plan of action.

Sample Development Plan Outline

Campaign:

  A. Goal:

  B. Participation Goals

    a. Board:

    b. Staff:

    c. Previous FY Donors:

  C. Campaign Objectives

  D. Funding Priorities

  E. Campaign Theme & Implementation

  F. Campaign Leadership

    a. Staff Roles & Responsibilities to Campaign

    b. Development Committee

      i. Role & Responsibilities

      ii. Chair: [name]

      iii. Committee Members: [names]

      iv. Meeting Schedule:

    c. Campaign Committee

      i. Role & Responsibilities

      ii. Chair: [name]

      iii. Committee Members: [names]

      iv. To be recruited by: [date]

      v. Meeting Schedule:

  G. Campaign Strategies [by constituent group]

    a. Board of Trustees:

      i. Communication Plan:

      ii. Solicitation Method(s):

    b. Staff:

      i. Communication Plan:

      ii. Solicitation Method(s):

    c. Previous FY Donors:

      i. Communication Plan:

   ii. Solicitation Method(s):

  d. LYBUNT/SYBUNT:

   i. Communication Plan:

   ii. Solicitation Method(s):

H. Stewardship Plans

  a. Giving Society Recognition Levels & Activities

  b. Gift/Pledge Acknowledgement Policy

  c. Pledge Reminder Policy

  d. Thank-you Plans

  e. Individual Major Donor Stewardship Plans

  f. Annual Report

Supplemental Development Plan Documents:

◆ Development Timeline by month/day and who's responsible

◆ Job Descriptions defining roles of committee chair(s) and members

◆ Range-of-Gifts Chart for capital and major gift campaigns

Chapter Four

Fundraising Methods by Rate of Return

IN THIS CHAPTER

- ┈➔ Not all solicitation methods are created equal.

- ┈➔ In-person solicitations are more effective than direct mail, telephoning, social media and crowdfunding, emailing, or events.

- ┈➔ The nonprofit leader's job is not just about asking but about acknowledging generosity.

The Personal Ask

The personal ask is your most potent fundraising tool. There are as many solicitation methods as there are ways to communicate, but they are not created equal. By far, the most powerful method of fundraising is a direct, in-person ask of a specific amount from a top executive or fundraising official to an individual.

A personal ask has a 50 percent chance of success. A prospect will tell you yes or no. You cannot ask for better odds than that. Nonprofit CEOs need to devote most of their fundraising time to making requests to major donors and prospects in person. Refer to Chapter Five, The Big Ask.

Stewardship

Fundraising is a relationship business. The nonprofit leader's job is not just about asking. Stewardship is equally, if not more, important. The development officer provides the executive director or CEO with acknowledgments to sign. Add personal notes to the acknowledgments directed to people you know.

Watch Out!

Dave's Experience:

"When I was leading a small nonprofit, where we had maybe a dozen donations each week, it was easy for me to add a personal note to each one. When I went to a larger organization where we had many more donations and signed dozens of letters each week, it was harder to keep up. At a minimum, a handwritten thank you or crossing out the formal salutation and replacing it with the first names of donors goes a long way in sending the message to the donor that they matter to you."

Keep a supply of birthday cards on hand. Send notes of sympathy when appropriate. Get to know your donors and their passions. Send along notes of common interest that can help strengthen the donor's relationship with the organization. Send congratulations if there is a significant event in the donor's life or an organizational activity worthy of mention. Little things mean a lot. Staying in touch with donors regularly, including calling just to check in on them, congratulating or offering condolences if appropriate, and updating them on the organization's success can mean a lot. Donors are much more likely to answer the phone or say yes to an in-person meeting when it's not always to be asked for money. By investing this time and energy now, it will result in more and larger gifts over time.

Telephone Solicitations Have a One-in-Four Success Rate

Telephone solicitations elicit a response rate of about 25 percent. That means that, overall, you can expect about one in four prospects to say yes, one to say no, one to say "I will consider," and one will likely be a wrong number. Moreover, with caller ID, many prospects do not even bother to answer the telephone.

After individual solicitations of your major gift prospects in person, more of your nonprofit's time should be spent in telephoning prospects and donors than in direct mail of your low to mid-level prospects. Volunteers, board members, and others can be engaged in raising funds by phone. Once a program has grown too large to handle internally, you can use paid telephone solicitors.

Provide callers with a telephone script or talking points. Including news about the organization's mission or work, the specific amount requested, and how the gift will be used are all-important elements of a phone solicitation.

Board Members' Calls Get Answered

When Dave was running a small, nonprofit law firm, the bulk of annual fund donations came in at the end of the year. There were far more donors than he could call by himself each December, most of whom were lawyers. Fortunately, many of his board members were also lawyers and from big firms. The donors were much more likely to take a call from a managing partner of a big law firm than from Dave. By equipping all of the board members with a script and asking them to make the calls from their personal mobile phones, nearly every call was answered or returned almost immediately, usually with a commitment to donate.

Callers also must be trained to have their remarks mirror the ask that may have also been in a direct mail appeal.

A combination of mail and phoning increases the response rate. If mail solicitations are sent in November, for example, make follow-up calls in December to those who have not yet responded. That will generate additional year-end gifts.

Direct Mail Can Net a One-in-Ten Response

Compared to personal solicitations and telephoning prospects, direct mail is the most expensive but the least effective fundraising method. You can expect a 3 to 10 percent response rate from a list of prospects who are already donors or at least familiar with your nonprofit. Some lists of less knowledgeable candidates and non-donors or purchased lists will generate less than a 1 percent response. However, direct mail is the best way to reach large numbers of prospects you will not be able to reach any other way.

Until your database reaches five thousand contacts, it is generally more cost-effective for mailings to be printed, addressed, and mailed from your organization's development office. You can enlist volunteers and staff members to help stuff envelopes.

Plan to send two direct mail solicitations each year (one in the spring and one in the fall) to all donors, prospects, and constituents. Otherwise, you run the risk of losing donors since the post office only keeps forwarded mailing addresses for six months. Do not mail too often or only when a goal has not been reached. Direct mail works best in conjunction with other methods of giving and as part of the overall development plan.

> ### Fundraising Principle
>
> A combination of mailing and phoning increases the response rate of a solicitation. We call that multi-channel marketing.

Solicitation Package Contents

Each solicitation package mailed should include a letter, a response device (ideally, a pledge form with pre-printed known information customized for the contact), and a return envelope. Postage-paid return envelopes increase the response rate. Make the body of the letter compelling. Include news about your organization, a specific request, and data on why the gift is meaningful and how it will be used. Create a sense of urgency by including deadlines suchas December 31 or the fiscal year-end.

Ask for a Specific Amount

An effective solicitation letter asks for a specific amount. The phrase, "Would you consider a gift of XYZ amount?" can be very effective. Base the amount of the request on the donor's prior year's giving. If you don't have a donor's giving history, you can also suggest the average annual fund gift or the average board gift, depending upon the audience. It is a good rule of thumb to ask for a 10 to 20 percent increase over the year before. This can be calculated into a specific ask that may be different for each prospect. You may also choose to ask for a range of gift amounts.

Fundraising Principle

Always ask donors for a specific amount.

Some organizations only ask for an increase every three years. In the other two years, they simply ask a donor to renew their annual gift at the same level of support. The letter signer can be you (the nonprofit leader), a board member, or a volunteer. Board or development committee names should be listed on the letterhead. The idea is for the recipient to be able to make a connection with someone listed in the mailing.

The two best times of the year to mail your solicitations are the day after Thanksgiving (or sooner, depending on the postage class) and on or around April 15. Research shows that donors are more generous at year-end/holiday times and at tax time. Donors have reviewed their finances and may be recipients of generous tax refunds that they are more likely to share.

Fundraising Principle

The best times of the year for direct mail are the day after Thanksgiving and on or around April 15.

Send the letters out first class if possible. First-class mailings generate a better response than other classes of postage. Include postage-paid envelopes as a response aid. Anything that makes it easier for the prospect to respond is worth the extra attention and expense.

After six weeks, conduct a solicitation analysis to test responsiveness. Be sure to keep accurate, up-to-date records of all solicitation activities over time. Record the dates of solicitation, the number of letters mailed, the total amount raised, the average gift, the range of gifts, etc. This takes the guesswork out of direct mail strategy and allows you to adjust future mailings based on the findings.

Email and Social Media Are Supplemental, Not Primary, Channels

Think about how easy it is to send an email. It is just as easy to delete an email, and it is the communication method most likely to become overused. Email can be used as a solicitation method, but very carefully, artfully, or only in conjunction

---

Stories from the Real World

A number of nonprofits dropped or reduced their direct mail programs after the economy declined in 2008 and again during the COVID-19 pandemic in 2020. Now they wonder why they aren't raising enough money. Do not fall into this trap when faced with budget cuts. And if you find your organization already has, take steps to bring back mail, but do it wisely, which includes personalizing solicitations with specific ask amounts.

---

with other fundraising techniques. It will likely become more important in the future and with younger donor populations, as will social media channels.

Like direct mail, email, and online giving channels work best in conjunction with other solicitation strategies. Given how rapidly technology and online channels evolve, they need to be consistently reevaluated for their return on investment in every campaign.

Many nonprofits have had success with personalized email solicitations. It is sometimes easier for board members and donors to spend thirty minutes sending personal emails to peers than for them to make themselves available for two hours of calls in the evening. Another benefit of email requests over direct mail requests is that emails may elicit an immediate response. That said, email is seldom effective as a standalone method; it works better when paired with other solicitation strategies.

Email Only Works Occasionally
Linda reports:
"The most money I ever raised from an email solicitation was a hundred thousand dollars. It was an anomaly. This particular situation was one in which we knew that the prospect really cared about our institution, but he was just too busy to meet. We had the board chair send the email with a specific ask for a hundred thousand dollars. We had our answer in a few minutes. Every now and then, it pays to take a bit of a risk."

Make Giving an Option via Your Website

It is surprising the number of nonprofits who make it hard (or impossible) to give online. Do not be one of them. Allow donors to donate online with a prominent button or tab on your homepage. A nonprofit must be prepared to accept cash, checks, and credit cards. There are costs involved with online gifts, but setup costs and fees can be offset by not sending pledge reminders.

Keep online giving level options low. Most major gifts are solicited in person and communicated through the nonprofit leader or the development office. Remember that a large contribution made online will be subject to a set percentage fee for the credit card processor.

The Importance of a Richly Detailed Donor Database

Logically, the more prospects you have to solicit, the more donors you can engage overtime. Use your sphere of influence to expand your organization's prospect database. Included in this database should ideally be all current board members, prior board members, everyone who has ever made a gift, and everyone you have ever solicited for a gift and event attendees. There is a tendency to overlook long-term supporters who may not have attended an event or given a gift recently. As a rule, if someone has ever been a donor to your organization, you should never delete them from your solicitation rolls. It is also true that once a donor, they may become a donor again, even if it has been a while since you last heard from them. Make it a habit to collect information about all visitors to your organization and events. Research shows that individuals that have been in your offices or seen your team in action are more likely to support your nonprofit, if asked.

Database entries should include the contact's name, salutation, address, telephone number(s), and email address. Don't forget to add notes on the contact's key interests, philanthropic history, etc. You or the administrative staff can add these notes. You should also document every gift individually, no matter how small.

> **Warning!**
>
> Never delete a donor's name and contact information from your database. If they ask to be removed, what they are asking for is that you stop contacting them for a donation. The best databases can mark that donor "Do Not Solicit" and repress them from database extracts. You never want to lose track of them.

The development department should solicit prospects by multiple appeal methods until they become donors or request to be unsubscribed or not solicited further. Once they become donors by some method, they can usually be renewed annually through direct mail or email solicitation. Then you can focus your fundraising efforts on *new* major gift prospects.

Think Twice about Special Event Fundraising

Boards and volunteers often default to events as their first fundraising vehicle. Although events are a great way to involve a large number of prospects, event fundraising is one of the least effective methods of raising funds.

When asked about events, Ailena immediately tries to talk a nonprofit out of doing them. Not because she dislikes them—quite the opposite, actually! Instead, her long experience in producing fundraising events has taught her that most nonprofits and their volunteers have little to no idea how much work it takes to pull them off effectively. Combined with a high rate of missing the unique opportunity to bridge the relationships built beyond the event, most nonprofits would fare much better focusing their limited resources elsewhere. Her reasoning is sound. When you look at the return on investment for the time and resources an event commands, the development department's time can almost always be more productive in other fundraising arenas. Here are a few rules of thumb when considering events:

Don't hold an event unless you are sure you won't lose money on it. An event should not be approved unless and until a detailed pro forma has been presented showing how much net profit the event is expected to make and from what sources.

Know your competition. No one will attend an event on Mother's Day, during the World Series, or when a British royal wedding is being telecast. Moreover, it is possible to offend donors with the insensitive placement of an event. Many nonprofits have found themselves apologizing to important donors for scheduling balls during the Jewish High Holy Days, Lunar New Year celebrations, or Ramadan.

Know what your target donors want. If the bulk of your donors make gifts of five hundred dollars or less, they will probably not pay ten thousand dollars for a table at a black-tie event.

Unique is better. In Atlanta, where the three of us live, you can attend a black-tie event practically every weekend. No one is clamoring for another. However, we also can be outside ten months of the year. Events that take advantage of that have a market advantage. Consider what will most appeal to your constituents instead of what seems to be successful for other nonprofits. For example, during the 2020 pandemic, events that could take place outdoors were markedly more successful than ones dependent upon indoors or virtual events.

Approach events as "friend-raisers." Strategically place staff around the ballroom, in activity groups, or along the golf course with the understanding that they are to connect with donors instead of just "working the event." Do research on attendees beforehand and have a shortlist of those you absolutely must meet or talk to before the event is over. Make sure to capture contact information for all attendees and send a personal follow-up to each after the event. And most importantly, find strategic ways to connect each event participant to your organization outside of the event. The goal is to build a new "friend," not just an annual event attendee.

Although events are a great way to involve a large number of prospects, event fundraising is one of the least effective methods of raising funds. However, events can be a highly effective "friend-raiser" and, if stewarded effectively, can turn event attendees into annual donors.

If a nonprofit is going to engage in event fundraising, pay close attention to the local school and community calendars and be mindful of how many competing events are held during a given year. Before deciding to hold a fundraising event, consider this: is it better to ask a donor for a thousand dollars outright, or is it better to host an event and charge a thousand dollars for a table of ten, netting only about seven hundred dollars after expenses of three hundred dollars or more are paid? In most cases, the outright ask is the better choice.

Event fundraising is also the riskiest of fundraising methods. A prime example is hosting a golf tournament that falls on a rainy day. Your event may fall on a day that coincides with another event that your donors/prospects will attend. No matter how great your event concept is, you are not going to lure donors away from the television on Super Bowl Sunday unless you are running a commercial.

If your organization does decide to host an event, revenue must be maximized. There are three ways to increase event revenue:

- Sell more tickets;

- Increase ticket prices; or

- Reduce expenses.

Board members and other good friends of the organization can and should purchase tickets to support the event. Complimentary tickets—"comps" should only be offered to sponsors at the top giving levels. Advance planning allows time for tickets to be sold. Consideration should be given to offering a discount if tickets are purchased well in advance of the event.

If possible, announce the following year's special event and date at your event if the event is to be repeated. Some events are successful each and every year. Be sure to track annual attendance and results. Some events outlive their usefulness and need to be refreshed or replaced with a new event or another fundraising method.

Gifts in Kind Can Reduce a Nonprofit's Expenses

A gift in kind is a voluntary contribution of goods or services. They can sometimes be converted to cash and may qualify as a charitable deduction for the person or company making the gift. Common gifts in kind include goods such as equipment, furniture, software, hardware, or vendor products such as food or printing. They can also include services such as a contractor's, lawyer's, or other professional's expertise; office or warehouse space; or administrative services.

> ### Gift Acceptance Policies Exist for a Reason
>
> Donors often look at nonprofits as a useful means to dispose of unwanted or fully depreciated assets, such as boats or timeshares. Expenses always accompany these. Dave remembers one nonprofit that he worked with that violated their own gift acceptance policy to accept the donation of a luxury condominium from a board member. The ensuing association fees that the organization incurred while trying to sell the property resulted in the organization significantly missing its budget goals for the year.

Gifts in kind can go a long way in alleviating expenses. For example, events held in private homes where hosts pay for food and beverages can significantly reduce expenses for your organization.

The IRS has specific regulations regarding gifts in kind. Have a board-approved gift acceptance policy in place that outlines the process an employee of your organization should follow when presented with a gift-in-kind opportunity. This policy will limit the liability that may inadvertently be assumed by placing value on gifts or accepting a gift that does not advance your nonprofit's mission or cannot be readily converted to cash. It further assures that a donor will receive timely acknowledgment of a contribution.

As always, donors should be encouraged to check with their own financial advisor about their personal giving and tax implications.

Suggested Gifts-in-Kind Policy

Your organization may accept contributions of goods or services that can be used to advance its mission or may be converted readily into cash. When accepting a gift in kind, the receiver must ask the donor to provide the in-kind donation value.

Linda remembers only one instance from her career as a fundraiser where she and her boss—the headmaster of a private school—disagreed over accepting a gift. One occurred when a major donor offered a gift she thought they should not accept. The donor wanted to fund a full-tuition scholarship for a student that the donor and his daughter would select. (The selection would be based on need and on the student's activities, not on the student's merit.)

What made the gift problematic was that the donor wanted to be able to select the recipient. The school did not make financial aid information public. There was even some concern that the gift would be taxable if such strings were attached to it. Linda and the headmaster proposed an alternative solution. They stipulated that the school would make the final selection for the scholarship recipient but suggested that the gift also include a one-thousand-dollar cash award in the field of interest of the donor's daughter. This gave the daughter input into the final selection of the award recipient and provided her with an avenue to have an educational relationship with award recipients. The school had several awards where the donors could be in touch with recipients and present the awards at the annual awards day. The final gift was much more than initially suggested. The award recipients and the school benefited, and the donor and the donor's daughter were more than satisfied.

The IRS allows an individual to deduct the fair market value, up to certain limits related to the type of organization donated to and the donor's income, of a donated item if it is kept by the nonprofit and used for one of its tax-exempt purposes. If the item is to be converted to cash, then the donor may claim a deduction of the cost value or the fair market value, whichever is less. *It is the sole responsibility of the donor to determine the value of a contributed item; your organization cannot assign a value to the donated item or services.*

Your nonprofit must enter the contribution in the donor database and issue an acknowledgment to the donor. The acknowledgment will contain only a description of the contribution and will not include a statement as to the value of the contribution. It will further contain a statement as to what, if any, goods or services were given in exchange for the contribution. Your organization cannot issue an acknowledgment for contributions that cannot be used or readily converted to cash.

For gifts with values exceeding five thousand dollars, the donor must complete all parts of IRS form 8283 and submit the form to your organization for signature. As the rule of thumb, the nonprofit's chief executive and one other officer—typically, the chief development officer, chief financial officer, or chief administrative officer—should be the only individuals authorized to sign 8283 forms.

If your organization has signed an IRS form 8283 and then sells, exchanges, or otherwise transfers the gift within two years from the date of the gift, your organization must file a donee information return, IRS form 8282, within 125 days of disposing of the gift in kind. Your nonprofit will need to advise the donor if such a transaction occurs as it may affect the charitable tax deduction for which the donor may qualify.

Beware of gifts with strings. There are occasions when you may decide not to accept a gift to your organization. In those cases, the development office should provide a letter of regret to the potential donor.

Grant Writing

Government and foundation grants are often the most unpredictable funding source, and each nonprofit must determine its eligibility based on the funder's criteria. For example, most independent schools are ineligible for government grants but may be eligible for many foundation grants. Approximately 15 percent of a nonprofit's development time and resources should be focused on foundation funding.

> ### Grant Funding is More than Grant Writing
>
> An effective proposal requires exceptional writing skills, attention to detail, knowledge of the funder's priorities, and a detailed understanding of the nonprofit's programs and metrics.

Although some organizations may employ a third-party grant writer, the development office staff typically write grant proposals. An effective proposal requires good writing skills, attention to detail, and knowledge of key programs and metrics.

Equally crucial to the grants process is accessing and managing the leader's calendar and essential volunteers. Relationships between board members and foundation representatives greatly enhance the likely success of foundation giving opportunities. A development officer can research foundation guidelines through online resources and websites. However, unsolicited proposals or proposals sent without prior communications with foundation offices are futile. It is well worth the time to request relationship information from board members and friends of the nonprofit to determine who has key foundation contacts.

Once those board/foundation relationships have been identified, a clear, concise communication between the foundation office and the nonprofit can be accomplished. Appropriate visits with foundation staff can be arranged with key staff and supporters and a gift requested within foundation guidelines. Once a donation has been received, make sure it is appropriately and graciously acknowledged in a timely fashion.

Foundation relationships do not stop with the acknowledgment letter. Most grants come with detailed reporting requirements. Most foundations are also nonprofits, and their executives have boards that they need to report to. Failure to provide documentation of how you used their funds to further your mission places the foundation staff in a difficult position with their boards. It may do irreparable damage to your organization's reputation with that funder and with others.

> ### Level of Corporate Support
>
> Depending on the level of corporate support, a benefits package may include employee admission or membership discounts, guest passes, event discounts, invitations to special events, educational programs for employees, and annual report/website recognition.

Most foundations do not underwrite daily operating expenses, preferring to focus on projects that create or innovate something new. As such, most nonprofits should not count on them for operating funds. However, it never hurts to ask.

Business Sponsorship

Sometimes a novice fundraiser will assume that since corporations have money, they might share it with nonprofits. Businesses, by their very nature, are in the profit-making business, and their gifts are usually given to receive something. More often than not, corporate philanthropy is seen as a form of advertising. Companies will sponsor nonprofits because they want to get their logos in front of potential customers, because they want to build social credits with their employees or communities, or (occasionally) to distract from controversial elements of their businesses.

On the next page is a sample of a sponsorship agreement between a nonprofit and a company that wishes to sponsor an event or program. It specifies the sponsorship amount as well as the benefits provided by the nonprofit.

A Final Observation

A nonprofit's fundraising plan should include scheduled direct mail, telephone, event, sponsorship,email, and personal solicitations. The effectiveness of all solicitations is enhanced with an accurate database and appropriate stewardship. The nonprofit leader will need to ensure that someone is designated to attend to details in the fundraising process and ensure that all laws are followed. The nonprofit leader needs to focus on asking for gifts in person.

To Recap

◆ The nonprofit leader should focus on asking for major gifts in person.

◆ Good stewardship begins with an accurate database and requires speedy acknowledgments.

◆ The overall fundraising plan should include direct mail, phoning, email, social media, events, company sponsorship, and grant writing by a team of staff and volunteers.

Company Name and Organization

[Your nonprofit] is pleased to confirm a sponsorship agreement with [company] in support of [program/event] which will be presented [dates/location].

[Company] has made/agrees to make a sponsorship gift of $_____ payable on [state the agreed-upon terms, e.g., one-time gift on a certain date or an initial amount followed by subsequent payments that will be completed by the opening of the event].

Sponsorship benefits are commensurate with the level of support provided and are often custom-designed to meet the [company's] particular marketing goals. [Your nonprofit] will provide the following benefits to the [company] in recognition of this support:

Recognition Onsite

- On-site signage
- On-site fliers or inclusion in programs
- Verbal recognition at the event
- Event title slide
- Donor wall

Marketing/Promotion

- Logo or text credit recognition in promotional and marketing materials distributed to database of approximately xx000
- Paid Advertising
- Logo or text credit recognition in paid advertising as available
- Press and Public Relations
- Text credit or verbal recognition in PR
- Events/Entertaining

Opportunity to host private event, rental fee waived. Please note that all direct costs (security, housekeeping, catering, and parking) are the sponsor's responsibility. Space available for groups from 10 to 300.

Tickets/Catalogs/Merchandise

- Complimentary tickets to the event; employee discount if appropriate
- Complimentary event materials
- Discounts on additional materials or shop purchases

Complimentary [level and number] tickets/materials for corporate executives

Agreed to and signed by:

Corporate Executive _____ Date _____

Your Nonprofit Leader _____ Date _____

Chapter Five

The Big Ask: Raising Major Gifts

IN THIS CHAPTER

- ···→ Why people donate money

- ···→ It is important to ask for support in person

- ···→ How to avoid common mistakes made by inexperienced solicitors

Fundraising is not a talent that comes naturally to most people. Most of us fear rejection. As an organization leader, however, you must talk about money—a lot. It helps to see fundraising as part of the larger cause, a means to a greater end. Think of it as the price you pay for the long-term commitment of those who care about your organization and its mission.

> **The Nonprofit CEO Must Know Fundraising**
>
> The CEO of the organization must be able to talk about money.

It helps to know the key reasons people donate money: they have money; they believe in your cause; they want to impact other people's lives; they trust the solicitor; their family has a tradition of giving back; the gift is tax-deductible. But the greatest reason people give money is because they are asked!

Where Do Philanthropic Dollars Come From?

Giving USA, the annual report on charitable giving in the United States, collaboratively produced by the Giving Institute and the Indiana University Lilly Family School of Philanthropy, provides excellent insight into giving trends that should be taken into account when considering your major donor prospects. Most novice fundraisers think large corporations such as The Coca-Cola Company or Delta Air Lines might be great sources for funding. While they are both generous donors, the *Giving USA* report tells us that corporations make up only 5 percent of annual donations. Foundations account for 15 percent of the total given each year. Individuals, on the other hand, donate a whopping 72 percent of charitable contributions. If you include bequests, which also come from individuals, 80 percent of the money given every year comes from individuals. The moral of this story? When soliciting funds for your organization, focus on *individuals.*

Types of Gifts

Annual Gifts: The lifeblood of any institution. They are typically unrestricted and used where the need is greatest. Everyone is an annual fund prospect and should be solicited for gifts every year. For further discussion of annual giving, see Chapter Seven.

Capital Gifts: Typically for bricks-and-mortar projects, such as a new building. See Chapter Eight for a discussion of capital campaigns.

Endowment Gifts: If annual gifts are like a checking account where dollars come in and are spent regularly, endowment gifts are like savings accounts. Endowment principal is usually not spent, but the income or a percentage of the income can be used for programs and activities. Endowments are especially helpful in years when giving is down. Endowments also demonstrate the institution's strength and allow for borrowing in times of need. The best way to grow an endowment is through planned giving, which is covered in Chapter Nine.

Major Gifts: Can be defined as annual, capital, or endowment gifts. They are just larger than usual gifts for annual support. They may or may not be given each year and sometimes are only received for special purposes. The definition of a major gift varies with each organization and can range from one thousand dollars to ten thousand dollars or more. Executive directors and CDOs should focus their efforts on major gift fundraising.

Identifying Your Prospects

The first step toward meeting the goal for major giving will be to identify your prospects. Because not every prospect can be expected to give or to give in the amount requested, the nonprofit needs three to four times the number of prospects for each of the required gifts in the gift table.

Your best prospects are previous donors. Approximately 80 percent of the money given to your organization will come from 20 percent of your donor population. Your fundraising efforts should focus on individuals usually in this order: board members, previous major donors, prospective major donors, all other previous donors, friends of the organization, and staff. Businesses, foundations, and other organizations can also be solicited but first focus on the top prospects in each constituency category. We believe that everyone is a prospect! Make sure to solicit all prior donors every year.

Sample Range-of-Gifts Table

Annual Campaign Goal: $2 Million

Number of Gifts	Size	Total	Cumulative	Percent (%)
1	$500,000	$500,000	$500,000	26%
1	$250,000	$250,000	$750,000	38%
2	$100,000	$200,000	$950,000	48%
8	$50,000	$400,000	$1,350,000	68%
12	$25,000	$300,000	$1,650,000	83%
24	$10,000	$240,000	$1,890,000	95%
Many	Under $10,000	$110,000	$2,000,000	100%

Prospect Screening

Rating and evaluating prospects on their capacity and inclination to give, and connectedness with the organization, is the next step in meeting your goal. If one does not already exist, create a systematic screening process that develops a well-researched list of prospective donors to complete the gift table. Prospects need to be rated on ability to give and interest and then assigned a contribution goal and timeline. This process will assist the board and staff in projecting how much money needs to be raised at various levels and the sources from which it will come.

Cultivation of Major Gift Prospects

There are many steps required to move a prospective donor toward making a major gift. Securing a major gift takes choosing the right time, the right person to ask, identifying the right ask amount, and the right motivation. See Chapter Two for information on the "Moves Management" process.

So, where do you begin? Start simply. Your first efforts at fundraising can begin with thank-you calls. These are a non-threatening type of personal contacts to make.

Consider the power of a personal visit. When Linda first started her fundraising career at her college, she visited every donor who gave

Why do People Give?

The greatest reason people give money is because they are asked. This is a core principle of fundraising.

at least one hundred dollars to the annual fund. She showed up in person to thank donors for their most recent gifts. Donors appreciated the personal contact so much, they sometimes got out their checkbooks and gave her another gift—and she didn't even have to ask! At her next job, also a college, the number of donors was larger, and she couldn't visit every one-hundred-dollar donor, so she visited every one-thousand-dollar donor. She tracked giving over time, which increased 350 percent from those donors who received a personal visit!

The amount of the gift doesn't matter. Pick whatever target works for your organization. Just make contact and get started!

The primary goal of a visit is to get the next gift. While you might start small until you become more comfortable talking about giving to your organization, your goal as a nonprofit leader is to raise major gifts for your mission. While you are visiting with a donor in a home or office, you can conduct your own research on the level of the prospect's giving capability and consider the appropriate amount to ask for on the next visit or follow-up.

Statistically, the average time between identifying a major-gift prospect and receiving a gift is usually eighteen months. The period in between is for relationship building. This cultivation period allows the prospect to get to know your organization, understand the mission, see connections between their values and the organization's work, and gain confidence in the organization leaders. Your role in cultivation is to help the prospect fully grasp the importance of the project for which you are raising funds. Treat the prospect like an insider through involvement and engagement.

> ### How Long Does it Take?
>
> On average, it takes eighteen months of cultivation to receive a major gift.

After the cultivation period, you will need to ask for a gift in person. Major gifts rarely arrive unsolicited.

Arranging the Meeting

People give to people. Letters, telephone calls, or casual encounters can only go so far. The best solicitations are conducted in person. Few people will refuse a visit if you have emphasized that a topic is too important to merely discuss by phone.

Landing the appointment for the ask is sometimes the hardest part of a solicitation. Making the appointment can be accomplished by a letter with a follow-up call, an email with a follow-up call, an email, or a telephone call. The message to convey is that this visit to the donor is so important and exciting that it deserves a face-to-face meeting.

> ### Who should Ask?
>
> Two solicitors are usually better than one.

You also need to consider who else, if anyone, should accompany you on the visit. Two solicitors can be better than one. Having a board member or staff member accompany you on a visit can make the importance of the visit more evident. It can also give you greater confidence.

Linda recalls that the largest number of individuals she ever took on a visit was five, and they got the result they wanted!

An appointment can take place in an office, home, or at a restaurant over breakfast or lunch. You can invite prospects to your office, but the prospect's home turf is ideal. Once the appointment is made, confirm it in writing.

Preparing for the Ask

Before the meeting, prepare a solicitation packet that includes the written case for support (see Chapter Three for more information), the ask letter stating the specific solicitation ask, and a pledge form. Review the case for support, as well as any supporting documents, to ensure you are well versed in the campaign. Practice a few times before the actual meeting. All major gift prospects deserve a strategy vetted by the development office and key volunteers who may know the prospect better than you. That first ask is usually a little unnerving. Once you have successfully closed your first ask, each solicitation experience that follows becomes easier. In fact, some organization leaders come to enjoy the process of soliciting major gifts for their beloved institution.

> ### Rehearsal is Not Just for Actors
>
> During her last campaign, Linda held solicitation practice sessions with the CEO of the organization, the campaign chair, and others involved in the ask the day before a call. They covered who would say what and when to say it. "Our merry band became so effective that we could rehearse in the car on the way to meet the prospect. And by the end of the campaign, we had so improved in our delivery, we could cover each other's roles."

The Ask

When you arrive at the meeting, take a few moments to establish a rapport. Look around the person's office or home and ask about photos or awards. Discuss a common point of interest, such as their affiliation with the organization as a volunteer or board member. If the prospect is a parent, make sure you know how their children are doing and whether there are any superlatives to mention.

When you begin your discussion in earnest, start by sharing positive organization news, perhaps a victory for one of the people you serve or recognition of staff in a local publication. Try to share something the person may not have heard any other way, or

> ### Put Your Money Where Your Mouth Is
>
> Make your own gift to the organization first. Nonprofit leaders must also be donors.

news not yet published. After you have made general comments, get right to the point of your visit. *"Would you consider supporting xx project at our facility?"*

In making the ask, your demeanor is more important than following an exact script. You must be passionate; you must express the importance of the gift; you must demonstrate your understanding of the prospect; and you must convey your confidence in the success of the campaign. Make sure that you have already made your own gift to the cause.

When you make the request, ask for a specific amount. Your advance preparation should have given you an indication of the prospect's capability, level of giving to similar projects, and the prospect's level of interest in your organization. Aim high. Prospects will not be insulted by being asked for too much. In a few cases, the prospect may give more than what was asked.

You Won't Insult the Prospect

Linda recalls, "I can think of no time in my career when a prospect was insulted or offended because the ask was too high."

You should mention that all board members and good friends of the organization are being asked to participate at a leadership level, and point out available recognition.

When ready, look the prospect in the eye and ask these three magic words: "Would you consider..."

"Would you consider a gift of $XXX for our YYY project?"

Then pause. Some novice solicitors jump in too quickly at this point in the conversation. Give the prospect time to think about what you are asking, and time to respond. Remember, this is a suggestion, not a demand. It sets expectations and is a starting point for further discussion. You are telling the prospect how to make a difference for your organization and how to fit into your campaign/ project.

Practical Advice

The three magic words to remember in a personal solicitation are "Would you consider...?"

Never Underestimate the Importance of Recognition

For some prospects, naming recognition will make a difference in the amount of their gifts. Some prospects will want recognition for their gifts. Some prefer to remain anonymous. You should be prepared with a list of options with giving levels clearly marked. Once donors sign

---

Donors Will Surprise You

Linda recalls she once had someone contact her office, and all she said was, "What do you get for $1 million?"

"I responded with three options, none of which interested the donor. Finally, I described the best naming option we had available from the recent capital campaign. When the donor asked, 'How much is that?' I said with trepidation, '$3 million.'"

The donor replied, "I'll take that one."

---

pledge cards or letters of intent, you will need to clarify the donor's wishes regarding the recognition options.

Anticipating the Prospect's Response

There are four possible outcomes to your solicitation.

Hopefully, the prospect will say yes, at which time you thank the prospect, confirm the details, leave, and follow up immediately with a personal letter of appreciation.

The prospect may say no. If this is the case, you will need to actively listen to their rationale, then restate their concern. Is it no to the project? No to the amount? No to the time? No to the organization in general? This line of questioning may lead to a negotiation.

Linda's personal mantra is "There is no such thing as 'no.'" Fundraising is all about getting the right person to ask the right prospect for the right amount of money for the right project at just the right time. If someone tells you no, it means *not yet.* It means you just have one of these elements wrong. Change things up and try again. And always continue to cultivate and practice good stewardship.

A third outcome might be, "I will think about it." Ask the prospect if you can provide additional information to help in decision making, and be sure to schedule a time to get back with the prospect. "May I follow up with you one week from today?"

The fourth possible outcome may be some objection, whether personal or otherwise. The prospect's personal circumstances will

> **Practical Advice**
>
> Anticipate possible objections to your request in advance and strategize answers.

sometimes preclude a gift. Either way, be prepared to answer all questions about the project. If you don't know the answer to a question, say so, and use it as an opportunity to return and provide more details.

As part of your initial preparation, you should anticipate possible objections and develop compelling answers with staff and/or volunteers in advance of the visit. When you hear an objection, it is important to listen actively and pause before responding. Restate what you hear for clarity and ask open-ended questions. In the end, summarize the positives and look for areas of agreement, acceptance, and interest.

Follow-up Actions

After the meeting, compare notes and results with the development team and other volunteers making similar calls. This is the time to make sure all solicitors are providing strong, consistent information about your organization.

You should have included a letter of intent or pledge form in your solicitation packet. It can be completed during the meeting or left behind with the prospect. Either way, you will need to follow up to receive the final commitment. In many cases, a written pledge to pay before the end of the fiscal year or campaign will satisfy your finance office.

If you did not obtain a firm commitment on the visit, follow up with a phone call a few days later and stay in touch until the pledge/gift is confirmed in writing. A verbal pledge should be confirmed with a letter (including a return envelope) sent in the next few days, specifying the payment details. It is best for the original solicitor to be the person to follow up to complete the gift.

If the solicitation is successful, always ask the prospect of others who might be interested in the project, and ask how would the prospect like to be involved in the project going forward. Often prospects warm up to the idea of participating in the project and then involve themselves in the campaign.

Recording details of the visit in person, or by phone or mail will help in planning for recognition activities and for future projects. If the solicitation answer was no due to objections, the prospect can be solicited again when their concerns have been alleviated.

Avoid These Common Mistakes

As a fundraiser, you should be optimistic, enthusiastic, and persistent. Don't fall victim to the most common pitfalls of soliciting:

◆ Not making your own gift first

◆ Not asking for a specific amount

◆ Not asking in person

◆ Not providing appropriate follow up

Comfortable relationships among solicitors and donors are helpful in moving donors from annual gifts to major gifts to ultimate gifts (bequests) for your organization.

The Steps for Cultivating and Soliciting a Major Gift

These steps outline the general process for cultivating and soliciting major gifts:

◆ Identify the critical few donors–those with the greatest capacity and interest to give.

◆ Familiarize yourself with the data available on your donors and prospects so that you can pull information in a useful format according to specified criteria.

◆ "Mine" (i.e. dig through available resources and data) for new prospects.

◆ Develop the relationships.

◆ Learn about the donors' interests.

◆ Share the story, mission, and vision, of the organization and the impact of their gift.

◆ Engage and involve the donors to increase their motivation.

◆ Discover influencers (board members, volunteers, friends, corporate leaders, etc.)

◆ Ask for a specific amount based on donor's capacity, values and motivation.

◆ Thank the donors for their gifts when they say yes.

◆ Try to keep prospects involved even if their current answer is no.

◆ Steward the gift in order to retain the donor.

◆ Demonstrate impact of the requested gift in writing.

◆ Continue to cultivate and increase the involvement of the donor in your organization.

◆ Review donor's satisfaction and interests: survey, evaluate and involve.

◆ Connect with other donors. Bring them into the family and the insiders' group by asking for their advice, involving them in decision-making, and engaging them in the institution outside of giving.

◆ Ask again for another gift (for another project, same project, another type of gift, bequest, etc.) Timing and relationships are pivotal.

To Recap

◆ The most common reason people give money is because they are asked.

◆ It takes practice to ask for a gift comfortably. Do your homework and take someone else along with you who knows the prospect too.

◆ It may take eighteen months to complete a major gift.

◆ Ask for a specific amount.

◆ Follow up regularly.

Chapter Six

A Primary Responsibility of the Board Is to Raise Money

IN THIS CHAPTER

···→ The ideal board has members who assist in fundraising for the organization.

···→ The development officer should have a strong working relationship with the development committee and all board members.

···→ Board members should be evaluated annually to include their fundraising efforts and results.

The primary responsibility of a nonprofit's board of directors is to advance the organization's mission. Not coincidentally, that is the same objective of fundraising campaigns.

This chapter provides important information to nonprofit leaders on how to build relationships with board members, volunteers, and donors.

> ### Relationships Matter
>
> The leadership team, including all development officers, should be encouraged to have strong relationships with board members.

Board members have legal and ethical duties as defined by the Internal Revenue Service and state laws. Additionally, the board of directors should be the nonprofit leader's most useful resource. Board seats are too valuable to be filled with poor performing directors. The National Council of Nonprofits has excellent guidelines regarding the proper selection and indoctrination of board members. Those details will not be covered here except to say a nonprofit must adhere to the highest standards in making board appointments. For our purposes, we will focus on the indoctrination of board members in their key role as leading fundraisers. How an organization handles the orientation of new board members has a critical impact on fundraising in both the short and long term.

Once board participation is secured, you can look to other constituents to help in development initiatives as well. This chapter discusses board, staff, and constituent involvement.

> ### Fundraising is Part of Board Ethics
>
> Board members should make your organization one of their top three giving priorities during their term of service.

As a nonprofit leader, you must cultivate a strong relationship with all board members, but your partnership with the board chair must be exceptionally strong. Just as you are the lead fundraiser for your organization, the board chair should be a primary fundraiser, too. The board chair does not necessarily make the largest contribution in any given year but should be a stretch giver. The board chair will be your partner in asking others to support the mission and as such, should be an enthusiastic donor.

CEOs should not feel threatened if others on the leadership team have close relationships with board members, officers or trustees; in fact, it should be encouraged. In order for major donors and supporters to feel connected to the organization, they need an entire network of strong relationships. The chief development officer, in particular, should have a close relationship with board members.

Every donor should have at least three relationships within the organization: the head of the nonprofit; a board member; and a member of the development team. This ensures if one of those individuals leaves the organization, those that remain can sustain the relationship with the donor.

Board Relations

Get to know the board members as individuals first and supporter second. Maintain open communication with each director on a regular basis, not just when you need them to perform a task. Know the preferred method of communication for each board member: email, phone, text, in person, etc. It helps to keep accurate records of their spouse and children's names, their office assistants and employees, and whether they prefer to be contacted at home or at work.

There are many thoughts regarding the "right size" for a board of directors. When asked, our answer is usually, "You want to be able to staff all the committees as laid out in the bylaws fairly and effectively." That could mean a board as small as five people or as large as eighty. We have generally found for most organizations large enough to have paid staff, a board of twenty to thirty members is sufficient. The goal is to maximize the number and diversity of the board members, and to increase the wealth and resources these board members represent for the group.

Annual Campaign

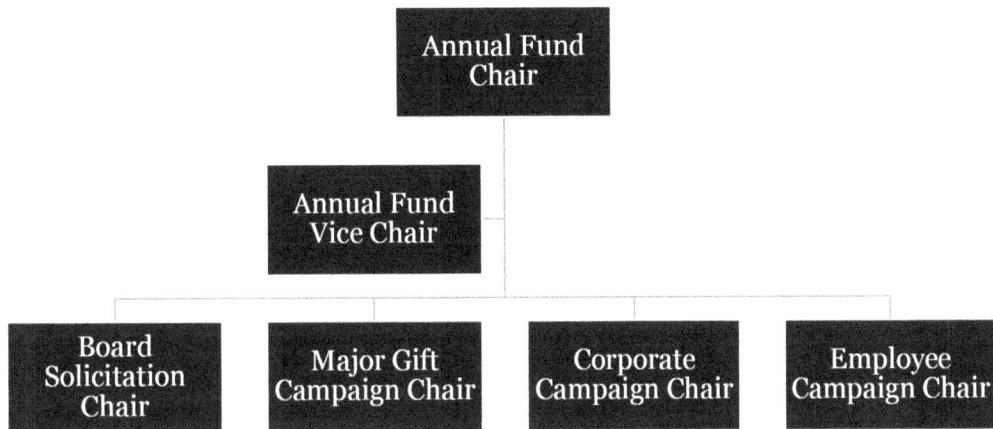

```
                    Annual Fund
                       Chair
                         |
                  Annual Fund
                   Vice Chair
                         |
   ┌────────────┬────────────┬────────────┐
   Board         Major Gift    Corporate     Employee
 Solicitation   Campaign Chair Campaign Chair Campaign Chair
   Chair
```

Board Member Self Evaluation

The following questions should be included in board member self-evaluations:

◆ Did I make the organization one of my top three giving priorities last year?

◆ Did I increase my annual giving? If not, when was the last time I increased my annual gift?

◆ Did I introduce any new prospective donors to the leader or to the director of development? Did I follow up personally with these prospects to talk about the future of the organization and to answer any questions?

◆ Did I personally thank donors this year, especially new donors?

◆ Have I considered a deferred gift or bequest? Have I discussed this with my financial advisor and family members?

Board Giving

All board members should be expected to increase their annual giving each year based on their abilities. It is crucial to clearly define giving expectations before and during orientation for new board members. Board bylaws should include the stated expectation board members make the nonprofit one of their top three philanthropic priorities during their term of service. Each new and returning board member should also be asked, in writing, to agree to support all fundraising initiatives of the organization during the length of their term of service, including the following:

◆ The annual fund (you may include an expected gift minimum.)

◆ A stretch commitment to any capital campaign.

◆ Participation in any board-endorsed fundraising drives or events.

Board membership should have term limits and members should be evaluated on their performance on an annual basis. The executive committee or a committee on trusteeship can conduct evaluations of the board members or they can individually conduct self-evaluations.

We are often asked to provide board governance training to boards of directors. Good board governance goes hand in hand with fundraising. Often, early in the training when we make that statement, a board member will raise a hand and say, "Oh no. You don't understand. This board *was never* meant to be a fundraising board."

We always reply to that, "No. *You* don't understand. *Every* board is a fundraising board."

Nonprofits are held in trust by their boards on behalf of the community. The laws and regulations which grant a nonprofit tax-exempt status also charge their boards with ensuring the organizations are well run and financially sound. It is both a legal and ethical duty of a board of directors as a whole, and of its individual members, to ensure fundraising is taking place.

Board officers should consider asking any non-donor board members to step down from the governance body. If the expertise of these individuals is needed, they can be asked to continue in an advisory or ad hoc role. All members of the governing board should be expected to make a financial gift to the organization, especially as it moves toward its next capital campaign.

All board members should be asked to contribute at least a particular dollar amount to the organization. If a board member is not capable of making a gift at that level, the board member should be encouraged to make a stretch commitment and to identify and solicit a gift of a minimum amount. Pledge payments should be made monthly or completed by the close of the fiscal year.

The board should always be solicited for their annual gift at the beginning of each fiscal year or at the beginning of each capital campaign. The development committee chair or another board member can chair the board solicitation campaign.

Board Solicitation Chair

Board solicitation chairs can be ineffective if they exert either too much influence or not enough. While you want to ask for a specific amount, no one should be *told* how much to give and each board member must give according to ability. Help the board solicitation chair understand the importance of the board role by providing a job description that includes qualifications, leadership characteristics and interpersonal skills. While there may be a tendency to assume that board members already know about the annual campaign, do not under any circumstances allow the board solicitation to be conducted through email or the mail. The board solicitation chair will need to lead by example, and ask for gifts of a specific amount, in person.

Board Solicitation Chair Job Description

Unwavering support from the board of directors is critical to the success of any nonprofit's annual or capital campaign. In fact, many foundations will not fund nonprofits that do not have 100% board participation in any campaign.

At the beginning of each fiscal year, individual board members will be solicited by a group of their peers. Specifically the board solicitation chair will:

- ◆ Make a personal pledge to the campaign.

- ◆ Recruit and solicit three to five board members to serve on the board solicitation committee. (These may be members of the development committee.)

- ◆ Help determine strategy for possible challenge gifts, prospect assignments, etc.

- ◆ Report to the board chair on board solicitation progress.

- ◆ Serve as a solicitor of other board gifts.

- ◆ Conduct the board solicitation campaign kick-off and report on progress at every meeting.

- ◆ Send thank-you notes for board gifts and pledges.

- ◆ Secure 100 percent participation from the board.

Develop qualified chair candidates by conducting annual board evaluations and having a clear system of succession. Future chairs may first serve in a chair-elect or vice-chair role.

This letter of intent can be amended slightly and used for other major prospects beyond the board.

Board of Directors Letter of Intent

[NONPROFIT] is grateful for the continued support and commitment of the dedicated members of the board of directors. Providing financial support, fiduciary oversight, and policy guidance are important roles of the board. This letter of intent is designed to assist you as plan your personal financial commitments to the nonprofit for the coming year.

Directors are expected to support the work of the organization through leadership gifts to the annual fund consistent with their means. At a minimum, directors are expected to make the organization one of their top three philanthropic priorities while serving on the board.

As plans for capital or endowment fundraising are developed and approved by the board, directors are expected to make leadership gifts to these to demonstrate the board's commitment to achieving the organization's goals. In addition, each trustee will be encouraged to make provision for the organization in their estate plan.

Your annual, membership, campaign and other gifts to [NONPROFIT] are critical to our success. Please use this letter of intent to indicate your proposed gifts for the fiscal year. Your early generous commitments will allow the organization to plan effectively and leverage other important gifts from throughout the community that will ensure our continued success.

Please sign and return this document by [X] date, or at the earliest possible time. Do not hesitate to contact the board chair, nonprofit leader or development director with any questions or concerns.

Thank you for your leadership and support.

Board of Directors Letter of Intent

Name_____

Signature_____

Address_____

City_____State_____Zip_____Email_____

Phone_____

In consideration of the gifts of others, I (we) subscribe the total sum of $_____ to be paid in the following installments: _____

Annual Fund_____

Event Sponsorship _____

In-Kind Support _____

Campaign Support _____

Program Support _____

Other Support_____

TOTAL _____

I (we) would like to complete my (our) pledge as follows:

Enclosed $_____.

Balance remaining $ _____.

Quarterly, beginning in 20_____, ending in_____20____,

Annually, beginning in_____ 20____,
ending in_____ 20____.

Other payment schedule _____

My (our) Annual Fund and/or Campaign gifts are eligible for matching gift funds through _____.

Thank you for your gift. In accordance with IRS regulations, paid annual and campaign gifts are tax deductible to the extent allowable by law. Please return this form to:

development director, address, phone, email.

Board of Director's Development Committee

The board of directors' development committee leads the board's participation in development and fundraising. The committee introduces prospects to the organization, solicits gifts, joins staff in making solicitations, and provides oversight, guidance, advice, and support for all aspects of the development program. That includes the review of policies, plans and procedures for fundraising efforts. The Development Committee Chair will be responsible for the orientation of new committee members, and will be an active advocate for and participant in all the nonprofit's fundraising efforts.

Scope of Work/Responsibilities

A development committee member will:

- ◆ Make a personal gift to the annual fund and to all major fundraising initiatives.

- ◆ Encourage 100 percent of board members to contribute to the annual giving campaign.

- ◆ Lead the board in their work to identify, contact, and solicit prospects for major gifts.

- ◆ Join the nonprofit leader and/or development director on solicitation calls to prospects.

- ◆ Provide advice and counsel for institutional fundraising (individuals, foundations and corporations).

- ◆ Be present at donor cultivation and other events.

- ◆ Set appropriate annual fundraising goals with development staff.

- ◆ Provide general advice and counsel to the development director as appropriate.

- ◆ Represent the nonprofit and its fundraising needs to the community and public.

- ◆ Review the annual development department plan and present that plan to the full board for approval.

- ◆ Review departmental procedures to ensure they meet current standards and best practices.

The development committee should meet at least quarterly. Specialized subcommittees may be appointed as appropriate to address specific purposes, and may have meetings in addition to the regularly scheduled meetings.

The board development committee should be made up of active solicitors who make leadership gifts and personally ask others outside the board to do so. It is possible to add non-board members to the development committee, but a board member usually chairs the committee.

To ensure that projects do not compete with each other for donor support, board members and leadership must clearly define philanthropic priorities for the organization. In defining these priorities, they will create a culture of philanthropic giving that may not have existed at the organization.

Major Gifts Training

One training method often used for governing boards is to role play various fundraising scenarios with trained development staff or outside counsel. Board members need to know that the most effective proposals are made face-to-face. Phone calls and letters are used for introductions, donation acknowledgements, gift appreciation, and follow-up communications. Board members should also learn the role of the development staff, who and when to contact, and how to work together for successful solicitations.

Sample scenarios board members can learn to address through role-play:

- How a board member can contact someone to make an appointment to talk about supporting the nonprofit

- How a board member and development staff work as a team to successfully ask for a gift from a prospective donor

- How a board member can talk to a close friend or acquaintance about supporting the nonprofit

- How a board member and development staff can handle a "difficult" prospect(hard to make contact, asks hard questions, grouchy personality, etc.)

Good Board Relationships Reap Financial Rewards

The largest check Linda ever received for an organization was from a board member. He had already made a seven-figure gift to the campaign, with an equal amount outstanding as a pledge. The payment terms were not recorded in the organization's database so early on she asked him the terms he preferred.

He angrily told her he would pay it when he "damn well pleased." He went on to say that when the rest of the campaign total was raised, he would give the final seven-figure amount.

The gift should not have been booked since it was conditional, so Linda forgot about it. Meanwhile, the fundraising team persevered with a very successful campaign. One night after a finance committee meeting, this same board member asked to stop by her office. It was late and Linda really just wanted to get home, but of course, she made the time to meet with him. Upon arriving at her office, he promptly wrote out a check for the full amount of his final pledge payment. As he handed it to her, he said, "Great job. I never thought you could do it!"

◆ What the board member and development staff can do if a proposal is turned down

◆ How board members and development staff can follow-up with a prospect after the proposal has been made

Board Involvement in Solicitation

Once the case statement has been written, the gift table has been created, the board is committed and trained, the prospects have been identified and rated, and the development communication has been coordinated, it is time to work the plan. Each solicitor team (board volunteer and staff member), will be given a solicitation kit, which may include a portfolio of assigned prospects with ask amounts, information on programs to target, and solicitation timelines.

Monthly evaluations of the progress will be compared to the gift table model and adjustments made accordingly. Along the way, donors will be thanked, recognized and engaged with the success of the nonprofit, and the goals for individual major giving can be increased year after year.

Nonprofits must have a formal process of approving fundraising initiatives, lest they get out of hand and actually impede gifts for the organization's top priorities. Beyond the annual fund and capital campaigns, nonprofits sometimes have special charitable interests or grant needs. The result can be a confusing number of initiatives competing for the same donor dollars. It is important for a policy to be in place mandating fundraising initiatives be approved in advance, preferably prior to the start of the fiscal year, and then at least peripherally overseen by the development officer. Approved fundraising events/activities should be added to the fiscal year calendar. Pop-up events should be discouraged as they can cause hard feelings and deter donors from making other significant gifts. Fundraising events should be limited to one or two per year, or a maximum of one per quarter.

Leadership Beyond the Board

Nonprofits sometimes choose to augment their board committees with community members outside of the board of directors. We strongly encourage this strategy. This move can serve to expand the community's involvement in the nonprofit.

Strong leadership is critical to fundraising success. It begins with the nonprofit's leader and the board of trustees, but can include individual donors, friends, experts in the field, and other stakeholders within the larger community.

Don't forget about your staff and constituents you serve. They can be invaluable as fundraisers.

Staff

Donors are eager to hear from the staff who actually deliver the nonprofit's mission. Combining the expertise and enthusiasm of frontline employees with the skills and resources of the development team is a sound strategy for deepening relationships with donors.

While engaging programmatic staff can be a good idea for fundraising, it can also become fairly complicated if those staff members seek to fund their own pet projects. It should be made perfectly clear to participating staff members that all solicitations, applications or requests for public or private gifts need to be coordinated through the development office. The nonprofit leader should reinforce this often.

Staff members who have ideas for funding are encouraged to discuss them with the development officer and/or prepare a brief written description of their proposal. Of course all plans for departments or programs need to be in keeping with the mission and strategic organizational goals. Seeing a proposal through to success typically involves extensive research, multiple proposal drafts, frequent communication with senior staff, and possible site visits.

If a proposal is determined to be a priority, the development staff can work with other staff members to identify and develop the relationships to qualify prospects, whether they be individuals, foundations or corporations. Staff may join in personal visits of prospects and prior donors; however, the development office is responsible for making sure no prospect is called upon too frequently, or simultaneously. The role of the staff member is to present the specific vision of the program to be funded. The development officer will provide guidance for follow-up and final submission.

The staff member alongside the development office will craft the tone and content and supporting materials. The goal is to design a message that defines how the donor's interests match up to the organization's priorities that enriches both parties.

The actual solicitation may include the staff member, the development officer, the nonprofit leader or others. Staff may also be included in stewardship with the donor after successful solicitations. Long-term relationships between staff and donors to the organization are both desired and mutually rewarding.

The development office must honor the needs and priorities of the organization as a whole. Some departments are more easily funded through private giving, while others are not nearly

---

Prevent Rogue Solicitations

Any staff member or volunteer can enhance the overall work of the development department. They can also, quite unwittingly, derail it. Dave remembers a time when he had arranged a luncheon with staff and board members to thank his organization's largest donor. Two years previously, the donor made a gift to buy and equip a mobile clinic and it was being premiered at the luncheon. The development team was also cultivating the donor for a similar, very large gift. During the lunch, however, a board member who volunteered in the clinic went rogue and asked the donor for a small amount to buy a single piece of equipment. The donor agreed on the spot. Unfortunately, it meant the development department had to wait nearly a year before making another ask.

so fundable. All staff can enhance the overall work of the development department by attending events, reviewing departmental publications and building meaningful relationships with donors and their families.

Constituents

For our purposes, we will define "constituents" as the people who benefit from the services provided by the organization. Certain individuals may be both beneficiaries of services and supporters. At a school, these would be the students; for a medical nonprofit, these would be patients; and for a performing arts nonprofit, these could be patrons and subscribers.

> ## Philanthropy is a Pleasant Psychological State
>
> Psychologist and researcher Martin Seligman asked his subjects to engage in one pleasurable activity and one philanthropic activity and then write about them both. According to the subjects' accounts, the pleasurable activity (watching a movie or eating out) paled in comparison to the philanthropic venture. Giving took the subjects outside themselves. Helping others had a stronger, more lasting impact than the more usual fun activity.

Many nonprofits struggle with constituent giving. For nonprofits who serve the financially challenged, one must shy away from the paradigm that recipients of the services will never be in a position to support the organization. If the nonprofit is doing its job well, hopefully those recipients will find themselves in a better position in the future to support the organization. Therefore, you should always include them in your database of prospective donors.

More importantly, who could be better to talk about the impact that your nonprofit makes than a recipient of those services? Involving those constituents in meetings and fundraising events lets current and potential donors learn firsthand the impact of their donations on the lives of others. Similarly, in nonprofit organizations like the performing arts, one must avoid the mistake of thinking that the role of marketing stops at creating a patron or subscriber. The goal of marketing is to create a donor.

> ## A Note on Marketing
>
> Many nonprofit boards and leaders make the mistake of believing marketing is separate from development. It is not. The role of marketing is, ultimately, to support revenue production through both the earned and contributed revenue streams. Marketing must support development and development must respect marketing's expertise.
>
> Dave recalls a time when a healthcare nonprofit he was associated with regularly ignored the marketing department's advice and placed large, four-color images of a badly diseased eye at the top of every mail and online solicitation. The campaigns were not successful, mostly because they were so visually startling. When the marketing department recrafted the solicitations to show happy children and adults in glasses, some of whom had been patients of the nonprofit, the campaign response rate tripled.

To Recap

◆ A primary responsibility of the board is to advance the mission of the organization by helping with fundraising: annual, capital and endowment.

◆ Collaborating with you as the nonprofit leader, board members must be willing to make the nonprofit one of their top three giving priorities and be willing to ask others to join them.

◆ The development officer should have a strong working relationship with the development committee and all board members.

◆ You must offer board members training and support and create a true partnership between you and your development office for fundraising. Board members should be evaluated annually to include their fundraising efforts and results.

Chapter Seven

Annual Funds are Essential. Not Sexy, but Essential.

IN THIS CHAPTER

- ◆ The importance of the annual fund to your organization

- ◆ Elements to include in your annual fund plan

- ◆ The importance of an annual report

Annual fund gifts are the lifeblood of any nonprofit. Typically *unrestricted,* they are used where the need is greatest. Annual funds do not finance new buildings. Annual funds do not create endowments. Annual funds do not usually provide enough resources to grow an institution.

Let's face it; it is just not as sexy to raise money to pay the light bill as it is to build a building.

Of all campaigns, annual funds are the least cost effective, especially if you are in the start-up phase. Well-established annual funds with a loyal donor base are less expensive. With new initiatives, the cost to educate and acquire a new donor may equal the amount of money raised in year one. The cost of raising a donor dollar is substantially less than raising a nondonor dollar.

Once donors make a first gift, they are likely to return as donors.

Each year the development team must motivate last year's annual donors to give again and to give at a higher rate. They must also try to attract new gifts and re-attract lapsed donors.

Successful annual fund drives should be planned at least one year in advance. The annual fund timeline must allow for the following:

◆ Board approval of the annual plan;

◆ Donor research and identification;

◆ Planned solicitation by categories;

◆ Volunteer recruitment and training;

◆ Special events;

◆ Follow up to solicitations; and

◆ Appropriate acknowledgement and stewardship.

When to Launch an Annual Fund

How do you know when you are ready for successful annual fundraising? The answer to that depends on the answers to several other questions.

◆ How long has your organization been in existence?

◆ What percentage of the annual budget is covered by other sources of revenue?

◆ Do you have a written strategic plan for the organization?

◆ Has the staff and board identified the organization's immediate and long-range needs (with accompanying costs) that justify fundraising?

◆ Is there a written case statement that describes those needs?

◆ Is there a written plan for annual fundraising and has it been approved by the board?

Fundraising Planning Requires Complex Math

Increasing fundraising is more complex than you might expect. Let's assume your objective is to increase the annual fund by 10 percent over the previous year.

If you raised $250,000 last year, the increase would be 10 percent x $250,000 or $25,000. The new goal would be $250,000 plus $25,000 for a total of $275,000.

However, if there was a one-time gift last year of $25,000 that will not be repeated, and if you normally have 1 percent gift attrition ($2,500), your starting point would be $222,500. You will actually need $52,500 in new gifts, not $25,000 to reach your new goal of $275,000 for the year.

In reality, you need a 21 percent increase to reach that ten percent improvement goal. Is a 21 percent increase in one year really attainable?

Sometimes it is advantageous for an organization to conduct a development assessment. In an assessment, an expert, usually from outside the organization, reviews past fundraising activities and makes recommendations for improvements. An analysis of where your gifts come from, what percentage of the budget is provided by the annual fund, and the costs per dollar raised are all measured.

Setting the Annual Fund Goal and Securing Leadership Commitment

If you have established that your organization is ready for an annual fund, based on a well-documented assessment of operating needs, you should begin by setting a conservative dollar goal for your annual fund. This dollar goal must be fully justified and obtainable.

You can base an annual fund goal on last year's fundraising totals with an increased percentage for this year. You must consider, however, if there were any one-time gifts that are not repeatable. Also, consider whether there is any possible impact from a special event or occasion that will not be repeated. There will be new donors and new prospects. Some of these factors can be planned for and should be taken into account when setting your annual fund goal. There may also be outside factors that cannot be predicted and can affect a possible campaign: news, politics, pandemic, scandal, etc.

Once your annual fund goal is determined, you must then obtain buy-in and a pledge of full support from key organization leadership. Board leadership and the head of the organization must fully embrace the annual fund. A 100 percent participation of the board in the annual fund is expected. That support must be formally demonstrated early and communicated publicly throughout the annual fund cycle.

Once the overall dollar goal is approved and committed to by top leadership, realistic and obtainable sub goals for each constituent group must be set, based on prior giving and reasonable incremental increases. All of the goals for the various constituency groups should total to more than the amount needed in the annual fund. That will allow for a bit of a cushion in case one or more groups do not meet their goals.

A budget for the annual fund must also be established and approved. For most organizations, the annual fund budget should be no more than 10 to 25 percent of the revenue raised in annual support. The budget must cover salaries, printing (stationery, brochures, annual report, reply cards, and envelopes), special events, premiums, recognition, phone solicitations, travel and ever-increasing postage and social media costs.

Establish the Annual Fund Chair and Committee

It is wise for organizations to enlist an overall annual fund volunteer chair. This key leader is usually a board member and a regular contributor to the annual fund at a leadership level. Their primary task will be to engage the other constituency groups and assist them in reaching their respective goals. The chart below, titled "Annual Campaign," shows the hierarchy of the annual fund committee.

The annual fund chair should be a major donor with visibility and stature in the organization's community. This individual will serve as chief spokesperson for the annual fund, sign appeals, identify and cultivate donors and personally call on a short list of prospects. It is customary to list each of these volunteer names on organization letterhead for solicitations and acknowledgements.

The annual fund vice-chair assists the chair and is in training to chair the annual campaign the following year.

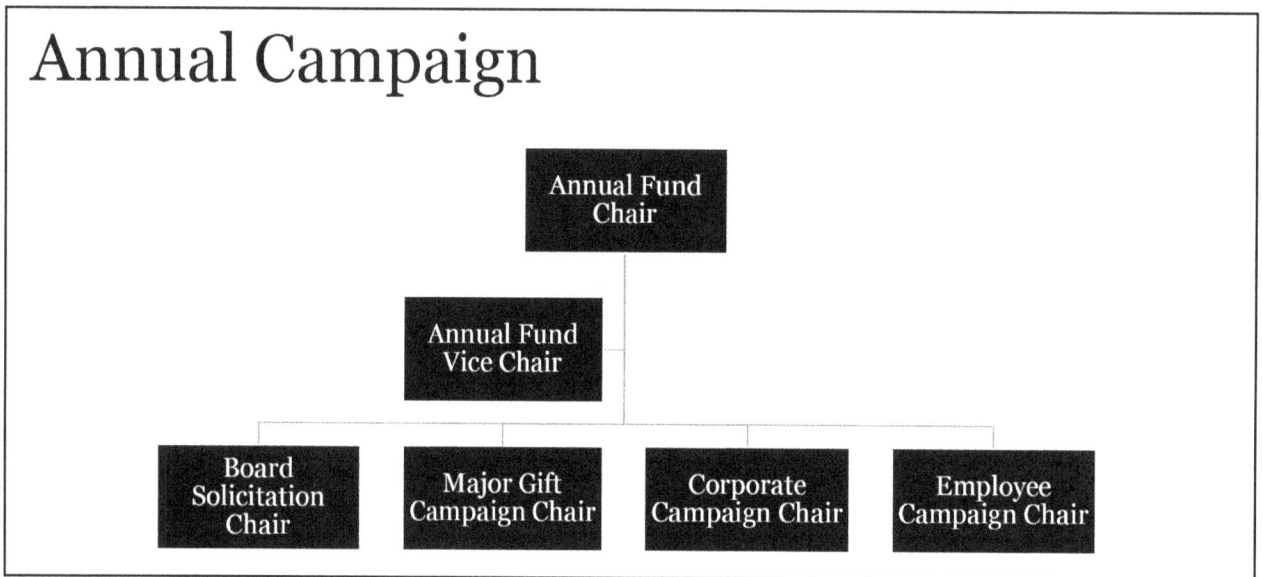

Annual Campaign

Annual Fund Chair

Annual Fund Vice Chair

Board Solicitation Chair | Major Gift Campaign Chair | Corporate Campaign Chair | Employee Campaign Chair

The development office and/or the annual fund chair should recruit these volunteers. Each volunteer should be trained in how to ask for gifts in person. If necessary, each constituency chair can recruit and train additional volunteers to serve on subcommittees who will solicit annual fund donations from each subgroup of their constituency.

The Annual Fund Plan

The annual fund plays a central role in the total development program. It is the building block upon which other funding rests. So whether you have a fledgling annual fund, your fund has reached a plateau, or you just need ideas to motivate staff and volunteers, your organization needs an annual plan. Use the following plan outline as your starting point:

I. Background . . . . . .

II. Objectives . . . . . .

III. Goals/Strategy . . . . . .

    A. Underlying Philosophy . . . . . .

    B. Defining the Prospect Pool . . . . . .

    C. Sequential Fundraising . . . . . .

The Nuts and Bolts of Acquiring Annual Fund Donations

Raising annual funds is not rocket science. The annual fund program can be divided into logical segments by giving level. This will allow you as a leader of the organization to focus on a few top donors while your staff or other volunteers give attention to the rest.

Acquiring Major Gifts

The success of your annual fund is largely dependent upon your success in acquiring major gifts. Major gifts are the largest gifts the organization receives and are typically significantly larger than the average gift, so they extend outside the normal fiscal year's fundraising cycle. Soliciting major gifts is time consuming: eighteen to twenty-four months is typical. As much as half of your goal could be expected to come in the form of a major gift.

 ◆ Define what a major gift is for your organization in terms of dollar amount.

 ◆ Develop a range-of-gifts table. (See example in Chapter Five.) This table documents the impact of different sized gifts on the organization's mission.

 ◆ Identify major donor prospects, segmenting them into renewing or new donors.

 ◆ Craft an individual strategy for each major gift prospect. (e.g., who should solicit the prospect and for what amount?)

 ◆ Assign five prospects to each solicitor.

 ◆ Secure 100 percent participation (in unrestricted dollars) from the board first.

 ◆ Secure a challenge gift/fund of at least $5,000. A challenge issued by a board member or other donor will motivate donors to give more because their gifts will be matched.

 ◆ Personally cultivate and solicit donors/prospects.

 ◆ Schedule personal solicitation visits with each major annual fund prospect.

Solicit Everyone and Establish Giving Levels

Individuals, as opposed to organizations, are the best prospects for annual gifts. All constituents in the organization's community should be solicited for annual fund gifts every year until a response is received. Once a donor makes a gift or declines, pull the prospect from solicitation until the beginning of the next fiscal year.

It is standard practice for organizations to establish giving levels or donor clubs to encourage giving at specific levels. Donors are incentivized to give at the level of their peers. A suggested breakdown might be as follows:

Annual Fund Giving Clubs

$5,000 & Above [Giving Club Name]

$2500-$4999 [Giving Club Name]

$1,000-$2499 [Giving Club Name]

$500-$999 [Giving Club Name]

$250-$499 [Giving Club Name]

$100-$249 [Giving Club Name]

Make it a practice to thank each donor within forty-eight hours of receipt of the gift. At the end of the campaign, donors and volunteers are also thanked publicly in the annual report.

Seek Tribute Gifts

Offer donors the opportunity to contribute to the organization in honor of or in memory of a friend or loved one.

Gifts in Honor: A donor can celebrate holidays, birthdays, anniversaries or any occasion with a gift to the organization in honor of a colleague, friend or family member. An honor gift is a unique way to recognize loved ones in a meaningful, creative way.

Gifts in Memory: A memorial gift celebrates the life of a friend or a loved one. The gift might be in appreciation of the loved one's devotion to nature, science, or culture, for example.

List tribute gift options in annual appeals, in special event mailings, and on the website. Personally recognize gifts of $25 or more with a letter to the family of the recipient.

Make it Easy to Give

There are many ways to make regular donations easier on the donors, including:

- Give volunteers and colleagues an annual fund calendar so they can follow progress and support the program.

- Offer payroll deduction as a giving option for staff. Include annual fund information and a response device in new employee orientation packets.

- Offer electronic funds transfer as a giving option. Larger gifts are possible if payments are spread over time.

- Offer a super easy online giving option. Make sure it works properly.

◆ Accept credit cards, PayPal, or a social media payments option for gift payments. Make it painless for donors. Some organizations have organization credit cards or affinity cards. Use organization affinity card lists and print free messages about giving back to the organization on cardholder statements.

Note: Some organizations balk at accepting American Express or Discover because those cards charge higher merchant fees. However, those cards also give higher rewards to their users. By accepting those cards, you enable the donor to reap an additional benefit from giving to you. It is worth paying that extra fee to make it easier for the donor.

◆ Include memorial and tribute giving options in materials.

Pursue Corporate Matching Gifts

Corporations and foundations sometimes make annual fund contributions to enhance their public presence and their employee benefits. Many employers offer a matching grant program that can double or triple an employee's gift. Constituents who work for matching companies are better annual fund prospects. They are more likely to give if you inform them their gift will be matched and the revenue will be increased for the annual fund.

To thank the corporation, an organization may offer event invitations and discounts, educational programs for employees, or annual report/website recognition.

Compelling Annual Fund Communications

Communicating with donors is important for good stewardship and building ongoing relationships with donors.

To be effective, annual fund letters must be personal and specific. Address the letter to an individual, not the masses. Consider starting the letter with a personal story that will hook the reader's interest. Avoid the theme of "we need your money."

In the body of the letter, tell the reader the dollar goal of the annual fund and be specific about how the dollars raised will be used.

Make sure to ask for a specific amount; this is sometimes done in the postscript. If it is a new prospect, you can suggest last year's average annual fund gift.

Make it easy for the reader to respond. Provide a return envelope and preprinted response device. Address the reply envelope to a specific person at your organization. While it might be tempting to save money by using postcards in lieu of letters, we do not recommend this as they provide no opportunity for a response.

Enhance the outer envelope with a tagline such as *"a message from the president"* for example, to increase interest in the letter.

Dear first name:

I hope you and your family are having a relaxing summer. It seems like only yesterday we were making plans for the summer, and now it is almost time to begin another fiscal year.

Thank you for your past support of xxx organization. As a member of the board of trustees, it is important that we continue to set an example for our staff and our constituents by contributing to the fundraising efforts here at xxx.

I am writing today to ask you to join me in making your contribution to the annual fund. Your leadership gift at [specific amount] will allow you membership in the roundtable of gift clubs at the XX Club level. Our goal is to raise $800,000 and to increase the number of donors in the XX Club.

As you know, the annual fund is the most vital fundraising effort at the organization. Your tax-deductible gift to the annual fund is used for... Your gift benefits all those we serve.

Enclosed, you will find a brochure and pledge card. Please respond by the end of the month so we can conclude the annual fund by the close of the fiscal year.

Thank you for all you do for xxx organization. Your commitment to the success of the organization makes xxx organization what it is today.

Sincerely,

Annual Fund Chair

Remember, major donors should be asked for a gift in-person, so the annual fund letter will be left behind after the meeting. However, with non-major donors, the ask letter may be mailed directly. Use first-class postage for the outgoing mailing whenever possible. It will be more likely to be opened.

Elements of a Strong Annual Report

Your successful annual fund drive will culminate in the publication of donors' names in an annual report. The report celebrates the success of the annual fund, illustrates the funds' impact on the organization community, and formally recognizes and thanks donors and volunteers. Think of it as a cultivation opportunity.

Include these elements in your annual report:

◆ An inspiring letter from the head of organization (written by or drafted for the head)

◆ One or more personal stories about how the annual fund is impacting the life of an individual or family served by your organization

◆ Inspirational stories about major or planned gifts

◆ Statement of revenue and expenditures

◆ Statistics on number of people served, number of donors, etc.

◆ Lists of donors by category

◆ Lists of board members and key staff

◆ A letter from the board chair and/or annual fund chair

◆ Future challenges and goals of the organization (plans for the next fundraising campaign)

◆ A response vehicle for those who want to send an extra gift or for those whose names were not listed in this annual report and who want to be included in the next issue

Some final observations

Annual fund dollars may be the most difficult dollars for an organization to raise, but this fund also provides meaningful involvement for new volunteers. It is a tried-and-true method of turning those same volunteers into future prospective board members. The annual fund also provides board and development committee members with experience in asking for major gifts, and identifies those who will not make personal solicitations.

The annual fund strengthens your connections with donors and enables you to communicate opportunities as well as your successes and needs. It creates a tradition of giving for families and lays the foundation for capital and endowment gifts. It is also a time for identifying, cultivating, and involving new prospects.

To Recap

◆ The annual fund is likely the most important fundraising effort at your organization and it comes around *every* year.

◆ It will be important that you and your development team set up and manage the annual fund carefully.

◆ You will need:

❖ A compelling case for operating support

- ❖ Trained and enthusiastic volunteer leaders

- ❖ A written plan of action for direct mail, telephoning, and personal solicitation of major gifts

- ◆ You must regularly practice good stewardship

- ◆ These efforts will enhance your ability to raise even larger gifts for capital projects and endowment in the future.

Chapter Eight

Preparing for a Capital Campaign

IN THIS CHAPTER

> ···→ The capital campaign process is ongoing, usually in three- to five-year cycles.

> ···→ The planning phase is critical to the process.

> ···→ Solicit in sequential order.

The success of a capital campaign lies in the details as much as in the dollars. In this chapter, we will review the important elements of pre-campaign planning, sequential fundraising, the role of leadership and the importance of stewardship.

The Timeline

While a typical capital campaign lasts an average of eighteen months, annual campaign activities occur over a three-to-five-year cycle. The first one to three years of the cycle includes creating (if one does not exist) or redefining the strategic and business plans as well as assessing staffing needs. It should also have a focus on the annual development plan, with intentional education and cultivation activities strategically geared towards the future capital campaign.

During the pre-campaign phase, typically lasting three to twelve months, detailed campaign planning occurs, including cost projections with architect and/or engineering plans, internal and external readiness assessments (e.g. the feasibility study) and the creation of the campaign plan and case for support. Following the feasibility study, another two to three months of campaign planning is common prior to the official launch of the campaign, to finalize any updates realized through the study.

Campaign Timeline

Pre-Campaign Planning
- Define goals & objectives
- Solidify strategic & business plans
- Assess internal preparedness
- Cultivate prospects
- Prepare budget
- Develop campaign plan
- Create policies
- Engage counsel

Silent/Quiet Phase
- Solicit board gifts
- Solicit committee gifts
- Solicit lead gifts
- Solicit major gifts
- Evaluate/revise goal

Public Phase
- Solicit low-mid level gifts
- Gain public buy-in
- Close campaign
- Victory celebration

3-12 Mo	2-3 Mo	6-12 Mo	3-4 Mo	3-6 Mo

Campaign Planning
- Revise/refine case for support & goal
- Revise/refine timeline, policies & donor recognition plans
- Secure board approval to move forward
- Recruit & train campaign committee

Stewardship
- Thank donors
- Hold naming ceremonies
- Install/unveil donor wall
- Collect pledges
- Campaign reporting

Feasibility Study (3 mo)
- Assesses internal & external preparedness
- Should be conducted by an independent consultant
- Makes recommendations for proceeding

Kick-Off
- 60% raised
- Official launch of the Public Phase
- Announce goal & percentage raised
- Media & publicity

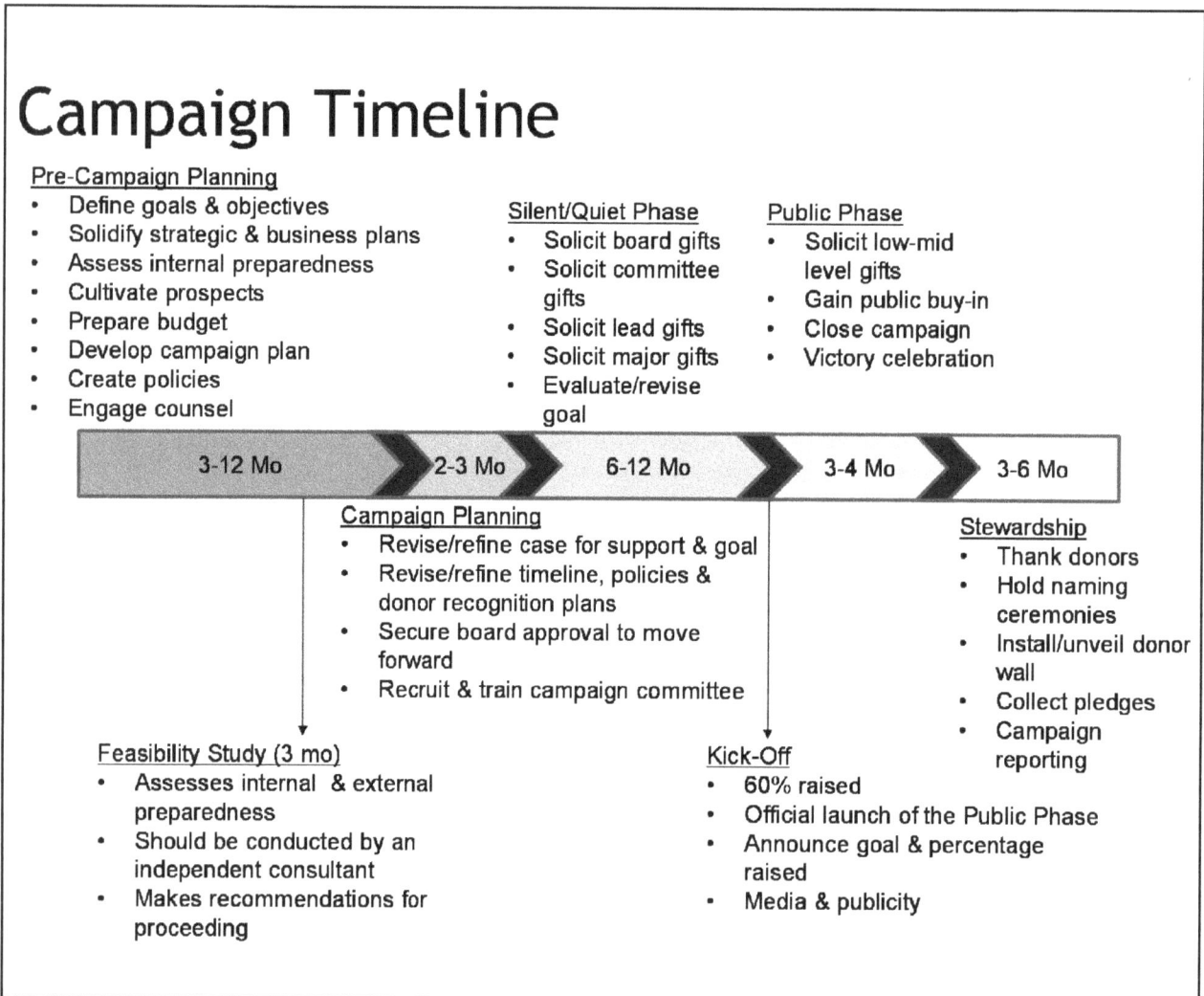

Once the active campaign is launched, fundraising occurs sequentially with the board solicitation first, followed by solicitation of your lead gift, top ten prospects, and then other major prospects. Always solicit the best prospects first, followed by the next best prospects. The public phase comes at the end when most of the money has been raised, allowing everyone to be a part of closing out the campaign.

Publicly celebrating the close of your campaign is important, followed by a year or two of collecting pledges and implementing donor stewardship.

Pre-Campaign Planning

As discussed in Chapter 3: *Three Secrets to Fundraising*, the keys to any campaign are a compelling case for support, committed leadership and a written plan of action. Those key elements for your capital campaign are solidified during this pre-campaign planning.

In a typical capital campaign, there are three distinct planning phases: pre-campaign planning (three to twelve months), the feasibility study (three to six months) and final campaign planning prior to launch (two to three months.)

It is common for a nonprofit board or leadership to decide a capital campaign is necessary and become so engrossed in the immediacy of the need that they rush through the planning process or assume it can be done simultaneously to raising major gifts. Do not fall victim to this way of thinking. The reality is the more prepared you and your nonprofit are for the campaign, even if the process takes a few more months than you would like, the more successful the campaign tends to be—and often leads to a shorter overall timeline.

> ### Three secrets to fundraising success
>
> As with all fundraising, the three secrets to fundraising success in a capital campaign are:
>
> ◆ A compelling case for support
>
> ◆ Strong leadership
>
> ◆ A written strategy/plan
>
> Leadership is the most important of the three keys to campaign fundraising success.

The pre-campaign planning phase is a time for questions, which should lead to the implementation of plans for answering those questions. What are the organization's immediate and long-term needs? Are costs firmly established? What will be the desired outcomes of these expenditures? Does the board agree with and understand the campaign process? How will the campaign affect the annual budget and the community it serves? Are there adequate staff and resources to operate a campaign? Is your donor community willing to support a campaign? If so, at what level of support and when? What is the specific project plan? (Usually there are more needs than funding permits, so priorities must be set.) What is the rationale or case for support of the priorities? What is the exact cost of each item in the plan? Is there a benefit to the donors/prospects as well as to the organization? What is the projected timeline? What will be the end results of a campaign?

The end of the campaign planning phase should result in defined goals for the campaign; a written plan of action including a timeline, ranked prospect list and range-of-gifts table; structured leadership including a campaign committee with written job descriptions; and a case for support.

Campaign Planning Checklist:

1. Updated Strategic Plan

2. Updated Business Plan

3. Defined Goals & Objectives for the Campaign

4. Cost Analysis of Proposed Campaign Projects with Input from Architect and/or Engineer

5. Assessment of Internal Preparedness for a Capital Campaign

6. Assessment of External Readiness (Feasibility Study)

7. Written Campaign Plan

8. Written Gift Acceptance Policy

9. Written Gift Acceptance Procedures

10. Campaign Budget

11. Engagement of Campaign Counsel

12. Written and Vetted Case for Support and other Campaign Materials

13. Established Naming Recognition

14. Board Approval of Campaign Plan

15. Recruitment and Training of Campaign Committee

Written Plan of Action

A written campaign plan requires self-discipline. While the Director of Development takes the lead in the creation and management of the plan, the Executive Director, Board of Directors, staff and volunteer leadership must both understand and buy in to the campaign plan. The process of physically writing out the plan identifies weaknesses and challenges of the campaign components. It also specifies who does what, when, where, why and how. When creating the plan for the capital campaign, carefully consider how it will affect the annual fund and other fundraising activities and how they will run simultaneously.

The Case for Support and Campaign Communications

The goal of campaign communications is to induce action. In order to do this effectively, you must know your donors and their motivations for giving. Campaign writing is not like other writing—it is highly personal and must persuade, show empathy, and then induce action.

The campaign solicitation packet will include the ask letter signed by the campaign chair and/or other leadership, the case for support relaying all major talking points related to the campaign, and a pledge form. The named gift opportunities should be available in solicitation meetings but not left behind.

When writing the case for support, make it long enough to explain why the dollars are needed, but short enough to keep the reader's attention by engaging your reader with examples and stories. Be clear about expected action; say it plainly, visualize and summarize, and clearly describe the campaign's goal and purpose. Include architect's renderings/floor plans/models and site or master plans to help donors visualize the campaign projects. Be sure to include a "frequently asked questions" section and a cost analysis that explains the goal. *See Chapter 3 for a more detailed description of writing a case for support.*

Whether it's the case for support or other marketing materials during the public phase of the campaign, tell donor stories, show how giving has helped, and feature campaign leadership, sharing why they chose to support the campaign. Let the organization's character shine through. Campaign objectives must be clear, simple and compelling.

Other campaign pieces include pledge forms, folders, stationery, envelopes, matching invitations to campaign events and newsletters. Digital versions should also be available.

Campaign Leadership

Campaigns begin with a solid base. The executive director and board of directors will provide the vision and mission for the organization, and the need and goals for a campaign. These should be clearly articulated in a written strategic and business plan. There should be openness about the financial health and track record of the organization. Financial information will need to be confidentially shared with individuals involved in the campaign. The executive director, board of directors and senior staff must participate in the campaign at a leadership level, including cultivating, soliciting and stewarding donors.

Board members play many roles in a campaign. Each can be the visionary, leader, advocate, donor, cultivator, solicitor and steward. The board must approve, understand and support the campaign plan. Like the annual campaign, 100 percent financial participation of the board early in the campaign is essential. Giving at a leadership level is also expected. Board members should be major donors, provide access to other donors and be willing to visit and ask. All board members should help solicit gifts.

> **Board Solicitation**
>
> Sequentially, solicitation of the board is the first step in the campaign. The board participation goal should always be 100 percent. Is a challenge gift possible—either in challenge to the board or from the board to other major donors to create momentum? Board members should always be solicited in person by their peer(s), no matter the size of their potential gifts.

The campaign director is either a staff member (e.g., the chief development officer) or hired counsel and manages the planning, coordination and execution of the campaign. The campaign coordinator is the staff member who supports the campaign director through the execution of day-to-day internal tasks.

The entire development staff should be well trained and familiar with the constituents. This begins with an accurate database and information must be readily available for staff and volunteer solicitors. Successful annual fund planning and solicitations will have prepared you and the development team for this step. Special consideration by leadership should be made regarding capacity of the current fundraising staff and department structure to take on a capital campaign in addition to all other day-to-day duties.

The campaign planning committee provides volunteer leadership during the pre-campaign planning phase. It is usually comprised of three to eight people, a volunteer committee chair, and key staff, and oversees the case development as well as the feasibility study process. The committee commits to two meetings—one prior to the start of the feasibility study, to approve the case for support and the list of proposed interviewees, and one at the end to receive the study findings. From there, the committee recommends the acceptance of the study findings and makes a motion to the board of directors on when, or if, to move forward with the campaign.

The campaign committee is typically comprised of ten to twelve volunteers plus key staff and commits to meeting monthly throughout the entirety of the active campaign. The number of committee members can be determined by the number of campaign prospects. A good rule of thumb is to have one solicitor for every five prospects. The campaign committee should be recruited by pulling from both the campaign planning committee and additional leadership volunteers identified during the feasibility study. The committee chair should be recruited first and then personally involved in the identification and recruitment of the additional members. Plan to incorporate fundraising training into the first committee meeting to ensure all members understand their role on the committee and are equally prepared for the solicitation process. Campaign committee members should cultivate, solicit and steward gifts, be part of evaluating the fundraising successes and challenges, and be truly involved in the campaign.

Typical Campaign Organization

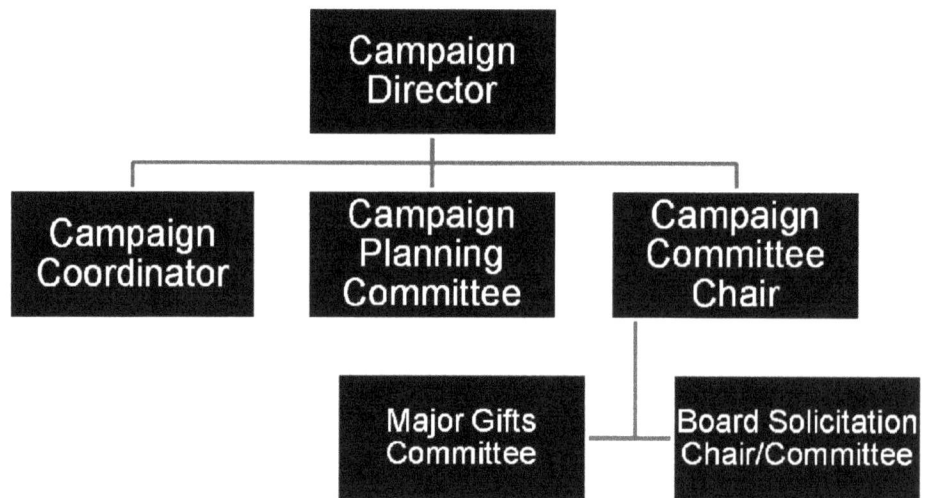

The development committee can support a campaign in several ways: they can serve as the campaign study committee members or approve members to serve; they can serve as all or a portion of the campaign committee.; they can hire and retain counsel; and they can educate the other board members about their roles as lead donors and solicitors.

All leadership roles in a campaign, both staff and volunteers, should have written job descriptions with clear expectations. Someone they cannot refuse should recruit volunteers in person.

Internal & External Assessment

An internal assessment looks at the internal preparedness of an organization and the resources needed to run a campaign. Some questions the assessment should answer are:

- What would be needed in terms of staffing and other support to overlay a campaign on an already functioning development operation?

- What additional resources are needed for the campaign to function properly?

- Are there policies and procedures in place that address situations encountered in a campaign?

An external assessment, typically referred to as a feasibility study, is the process of assessing the likelihood of an organization's top prospects to support a campaign and at what financial level. The goals of the feasibility study are to:

- determine the potential of your organization for raising the major gifts needed for a successful campaign;

- identify the top ten gifts;

- identify campaign leadership; and

- determine the approximate amount that can be raised.

Prior to a nonprofit committing to a campaign, a third party typically conducts the feasibility study. The study is based on objective, personal interviews with top potential prospects, and

---

Why Hire Counsel?

We are often asked about the role of counsel during a campaign. Counsel can help guide each stage of the process, identify red flags, and help you avoid costly detours. Counsel also offers objectivity and experience, and can provide training for staff and volunteers. Sometimes, your board may just need to hear feedback from an outside source. Counsel can be most useful if your development team or key volunteers have limited campaign experience.

usually takes three to six months, but timing depends on the development of the case for support and the availability of interviewees. The cost of a study depends on the number of interviews conducted and the geographical location of interviewees.

Why hire outside counsel for a feasibility study when you've spent countless hours building relationships with these same individuals? Wouldn't your relationship with them make you the obvious choice to ask their opinion?

Maybe, but outside counselors can be good listeners and strategists, and can often elicit information interviewees are hesitant to share with staff or a board member. They may not want to hurt your feelings or appear to be non-supportive and may (and in our experience...often) hold back information that would help craft the most successful campaign plan.

The results of the feasibility study help fine-tune the campaign plan, case for support and goal(s) of the campaign. Analysis and recommendations are provided in a final report and plan of action.

Pre-Launch Planning

The feasibility study often identifies items that need to be addressed prior to launching the campaign. This might be as small as tweaks to the case for support for added clarity, or as big as addressing donor concerns about any number of things. The length of the final campaign planning phase will depend entirely on the work put in up to this point, as well as the findings identified during the feasibility study and the length of time needed to address them.

This is the time to ensure that all systems and processes for accepting pledges, processing gifts, and the acknowledgement of those pledges/gifts are in place.

> **Stories from the Real World**
>
> Linda always keeps a list of named spaces at her institution easily accessible, as well as a list of approved naming opportunities. Once, a guest stopped her and asked for help locating her Great Aunt Susie's named room. None of the current staff could help and they had to go on a hunt to find the room. Embarrassed, she quickly remedied that with a list of named spaces distributed to staff.

Define gift-naming opportunities. These can include buildings, rooms, a donor wall, time-limited named spaces, named endowment funds, or expendable named program funds. You should have a list of all available naming opportunities to share in solicitation meetings. These include all potential spaces/programs to be named, not just those associated with the current campaign.

Campaign Launch

Congratulations—you've made it! You put in the time to properly prepare a solid plan and timeline; the feasibility study is complete and recommends that you move forward; and you have recruited and trained the campaign committee. You have now reached the active phase of the campaign.

The active phase actually includes two phases: the silent/quiet phase, during which you solicit all major gifts; and the public phase, when you launch the full-scale marketing campaign to invite everyone to participate. The majority of the funds raised in the campaign will be raised during the silent phase, so resist the urge to publicly market the campaign too early.

> ### Sequential Fundraising
>
> Sequential fundraising is the process of ranking prospects by gift ability and soliciting for donations from the top down.

A proven method of successful campaign soliciting is called sequential fundraising, which simply means ranking prospects by ability and likelihood of a gift and making asks in that order.

Sequential fundraising asks:

1. Board of Directors (100 percent before active campaign)

2. Campaign Committee Chair & Members (100 percent before active campaign)

3. Lead Gift

4. Top Ten Major Gifts

5. Other Major Gifts

6. Everyone Else (i.e., the public phase)

Once all major gift prospects have been solicited AND the campaign has secured between 60 and 80 percent of the goal, leadership can make the decision to launch the public phase of the campaign. The public phase is the point of the campaign in which widespread visibility is brought to the campaign. Public gifts typically equate to less than 10 percent of the campaign goal.

The Range-of-Gifts Table

A range-of-gifts table provides you with the—you guessed it—range of gifts and number of prospects needed in order to meet the campaign goal. A range-of-gifts table educates the campaign leadership about expected gift size, informs prospective donors, and focuses all campaign workers on soliciting in sequential order—the top ten gifts first.

In developing a range-of-gifts table, the lead gift needed is usually about 20 percent of the total goal. The top ten to thirty gifts usually make up about one-half of the campaign total. All gifts solicited during the silent phase of the campaign are major gift prospects and should be asked personally. A version of the range-of-gifts table can be created that translates the suggested number of gifts (first column in the sample chart) into prospect names to be assigned to solicitors. Usually, the larger the campaign, the longer the top-gift phase and the higher the dollar value of the amount to be raised.

Sample Range-of-Gifts Table

Campaign Goal: $10 Million

No. of Gifts	Size	Total	Cumulative	Percent (%)
1	$2,000,000	$2,000,000	$2,000,000	20%
1	$1,000,000	$1,000,000	$3,000,000	30%
3	$500,000	$1,500,000	$4,500,000	45%
5	$250,000	$1,250,000	$5,750,000	57%
10	$100,000	$1,000,000	$6,750,000	67%
20	$50,000	$1,000,000	$7,750,000	77%
40	$25,000	$1,000,000	$8,750,000	87%
60	$10,000	$600,000	$9,350,000	93%
Many	Under $10,000	$650,000	$10,000,000	100%

Campaign Committee

The campaign committee should personally solicit gifts and provide insight for solicitation strategies, as well as motivate other volunteers and campaign leadership. The development staff should handle the rest of the details. The campaign will continue to move forward if the campaign committee practices intentional contacts, cultivation, solicitation, and closing. When one action closes, another opens. The committee should meet regularly and use email and voicemail as tools in between.

The development office should prepare written talking points, solicitation materials, proposals, draft all correspondence, coordinate meetings, and handle solicitation tracking for the committee. An action item report should include the prospect name, the projected ask amount, the assigned solicitor and staff back up, the last action date, and the next step and date.

The Annual Fund during a Capital Campaign

Before launching a capital campaign, decide how to integrate or separate annual fund/operating campaigns and capital campaign priorities. Joint asks for major donors and prospects are often used. It is possible to grow the annual fund during a capital campaign by using multi-year annual fund pledges, challenge grants, and marketing membership in annual giving societies. Social media is most useful to a campaign during the public phase.

Celebration

It is important to officially end the campaign by holding a victory celebration for volunteers and donors. Write donors to let them know that the campaign goal has been reached, and seek ways to keep volunteers/donors involved in new activities. It's essential to provide any and all donor recognition and signage that was promised, and be creative and sincere in all correspondence.

Stewardship

Stewardship is the act of showing appreciation for the contributions of donors and volunteers. It is both immediate and ongoing.

Immediate stewardship includes a written acknowledgement of the gift or pledge within twenty-four hours. It includes personal notes and/or phone calls from campaign leadership to say thank you, and also includes keeping the donor informed of updates and milestones reached throughout the campaign. You must do what you promised you would do when you presented them with your case for support. Collect the pledges and communicate campaign results with your donors. Pledge reminders should be sent at appropriate times throughout the campaign, avoiding window envelopes or something that looks like an invoice. Form letters should not replace relationships and relationship building. Personalized pledge reminders, with telephone calls, are another cultivation opportunity, and each pledge payment should be treated as a new gift.

Ongoing stewardship will occur for three to five years following the campaign, which is not only important to the current campaign but to future campaigns as well. An individual stewardship plan should be created for each major campaign donor, outlining how you will continue to cultivate an intentional relationship and engage them in the organization for years to come.

The Cycle Starts Again

Closing the campaign well sets you up for a successful next campaign. Preparation for the next campaign should begin immediately, but not before a final analysis of the last campaign. The campaign plan should be evaluated and updated. Final financial and donor reports should be prepared, and cash flow reports that detail pledge payments should be provided. Review all open pledges and any necessary write offs, and analyze all refusals and any prospects that did not yet make commitments. Follow up on any outstanding gift opportunities, and make recommendations for improvements in the next campaign while campaign activities are fresh in mind.

Characteristics of a Successful Campaign

Successful campaigns have the following characteristics:

◆ Written, strategic campaign plan

◆ Strong leadership with defined roles

◆ Follow the principle of sequential fundraising

◆ Personal solicitations

◆ Specific ask amounts

◆ One hundred percent board support

◆ Trained, experienced staff

◆ A budget of 3 to 5 percent of the amount to be raised

◆ Counsel

Top mistakes made in Capital Campaigns

There are many ways to damage a campaign. These are the most frequent ones:

◆ Speeding through the planning phase

◆ Announcing the campaign prematurely

◆ Lack of defined leadership roles

◆ No, or too few, committee meetings

◆ Not asking for specific amounts

◆ Not asking in person

◆ Too much dependence on one donor

◆ Lack of follow-through to close gifts

To Recap

◆ The process can take up to five years with good planning and includes cultivation and stewardship.

◆ The planning phase is crucial to the process and should not be skipped or rushed.

◆ The majority of the active campaign will be spent in the silent phase with leadership personally soliciting prospects in sequential order.

◆ Celebrate the campaign's success, evaluate, and then start the process again.

Chapter Nine

Endowment Building

IN THIS CHAPTER

···→ An endowment is a legal structure for a set of financial investments that generate income for a nonprofit. An endowment is critical to the long-term financial success of a nonprofit.

···→ Build an endowment after you have secured your annual fundraising base of support and satisfied immediate capital needs.

···→ Initiate a planned giving program and educate all of your constituents.

An endowment is a legal structure for managing, and in many cases indefinitely perpetuating, a pool of financial, real estate, or other investments for a specific purpose, according to the will of its founders and donors. For nonprofits, an endowment typically begins as a donation of money, investments or property to the organization, which then uses the resulting income for a specific purpose. An endowment can also refer to the total of a nonprofit institution's investable assets, also known as its principal or corpus, which is meant to be used for operations or programs consistent with the wishes of the donor(s). Most nonprofits' endowments

---

Key Endowment Facts

◆ Most endowments are designed to keep the principal amount, known as the corpus, intact while using the investment income for charitable efforts or operations.

◆ Endowments tend to be organized as a trust, a private foundation, or a public charity.

◆ Educational institutions, cultural institutions, and service-oriented organizations typically have endowments.

are designed to keep the principal amount intact while using the investment income for charitable efforts or operations. This chapter focuses on how to create and build an endowment through planned giving and education of your constituency groups.

Should You Have an Endowment?

There are varying opinions among nonprofit leaders regarding the value of endowments. We are strong proponents of them. An endowment is critical for providing long-term stability for any nonprofit.

In March 2020, Andrew Lo, Egor Matveyev and Stefan Zeume published a study titled "The Risk, Reward, and Asset Allocation of Nonprofit Endowment Funds." The study evaluated the asset allocation decisions and returns of endowment funds of the entire nonprofit sector in the United States. Their data was collected directly from the tax forms filed by nonprofits with the U.S. Internal Revenue Service, and their study contained all nonprofits with established endowments between the years 2009 and 2017. Some of their findings were as follows:

◆ The average endowment fund had $20.5 million in assets under management (AUM), largely driven by a few very large funds, as the median AUM was under $1 million.

◆ Endowments in higher education accounted for a mere 3.7 percent of all endowment funds, but their assets accounted for almost 40 percent.

◆ The average return on invested capital, net of administrative expenses, was 5.3 percent.

◆ The average administrative expenses were 1 percent of AUM annually.

◆ Large endowment funds significantly outperformed small funds, both in terms of returns and risk-adjusted returns. In particular, funds with more than $100 million in AUM had average net returns of 7.6 percent per year, while funds with an AUM below $1 million had returns of only 3.8 percent per year. Some, but not all, of the difference is explained by asset allocation, as smaller endowment funds allocated a disproportionately large fraction of their portfolios in fixed income and cash instruments—on average, almost a third.

◆ Board independence has a strong positive relationship to investment returns. Said plainly, the less ability the board has to interfere with the management of the fund, the better it performs.

While some nonprofit leaders believe the money in an endowment could be better used for immediate needs, we prefer the long-term view. Endowments mitigate risk and enable organizations to navigate unforeseen circumstances. During the 2008 recession and 2020 pandemic, many nonprofits survived only because of their endowments.

What is the optimum size of an endowment? Guidestar's guidance is, at a minimum, it should be two times the amount of your annual budget; for example, if your annual budget is

$2 million, your endowment should be $4 million. Some say the optimum size for a nonprofit's endowment is three to five times its annual budget. Obviously, the larger the endowment, the more financial security the nonprofit enjoys.

As the nonprofit leader, it is implicit you know what the market value of your endowment is, how many endowment funds you have, what their investment strategy is, and how they are governed and managed. Once you know these things, you can plan for the endowment's future.

Whether you have an endowment already or are starting from scratch, you know you are ready for endowment building when you have defined your mission, have a solid financial base, a growing donor pool, and the highest quality product in which donors can invest. As with any other type of campaign, the leadership team needs to be committed to an endowment for fundraising to be successful. It helps to have a long-term history of annual giving to allow you to profile and prospect among annual donors. And there always needs to be a balance between asking for operating, endowment and capital needs.

Creating a Planned Giving Program

The best way to create or build an endowment is through planned giving.

Planned gifts are generally defined as charitable gift instruments that transfer assets to the organization for current use, including bequests in wills, charitable gift annuities, charitable trusts, life insurance policies, real estate and split-interest gifts. These gift arrangements often have special tax benefits to the donor and allow gifts of accumulated assets at the end of the donor's life, or at a time most beneficial to the donor. The good news is you do not have to be an expert in planned giving to begin a planned giving program.

The organization will need to set up an endowment account(s) with a local bank or investment firm. The board will need to be committed to building a stream of secure, continuous earnings from the endowment through a sound investment strategy. This, in turn, will provide predictable dollar support of the annual operating budget. In other words, the investment of the endowment funds must ensure continuing income support of operations. The board will need to manage the risk and set financial targets. Most nonprofits set a goal of 5 percent annual return over the long term. Some use a three- to five-year rolling average to calculate spending.

Here is an example of how to calculate Fair Market Value (FMV): add up the FMV of the fund on a certain date for the last five years (2021, 2020, 2019, 2018, 2017) and divide by five to get the average FMV over those five years. Then multiply the percentage you spent of that average FMV. This averages the value of the fund so that you do not overspend in a year the fund has high market value, or find yourself underfunded in a bad earnings year. Spending averages out as the market fluctuates.

The board will need to engage an endowment investment manager working in conjunction with the finance and/or investment committees of the board to manage the funds, enforce the policies, and monitor spending along with the nonprofit's CFO.

The first step to creating a planned giving program is to craft a compelling case for endowment, conveying a sense of urgency and explaining the impact of endowment growth. You must engage leadership, then draft an endowment plan or strategy.

Do you know how many planned giving commitments your organization has already? Chances are, you may have some you aren't even aware of because they are buried in finance or fundraising files. We have found a number of these documents just by reading institutional paper files and talking to long-time staff members.

Beyond the commitments you already have, who are your best prospects and what is the best strategy to connect with them?

Planned Giving Requires Good Record Keeping

Turnover in development staff sometimes causes planned gift donors to become lost or neglected over time. This is only solved by ensuring an organization has a solid donor documentation system and strict adherence to policies on how to use it.

Someone will need to do the research first, likely the development officer. Some nonprofits hire dedicated planned giving officers. If you do hire a person dedicated to planned giving, it will be important to manage your expectations in the beginning. Many organizations have had start-and-stop programs because there were no realized planned gifts in the first years. Planned giving is a long-term solution to your endowment funding. There must be clear expectations among your board and leaders before initiating a planned giving program. It may take five or more years before a planned giving campaign realizes its first gift.

◆ Some questions to ask as you build or revive your planned giving program:

◆ What is the total of realized bequests your nonprofit has received to date?

◆ Has this number of bequests been tracked over time?

◆ What is the average bequest gift that has been received?

◆ What is the total lifetime gift from bequest donors that has come to your organization?

◆ What is the ratio of bequest gifts to lifetime gifts for your donor(s)?

◆ What is the percent of bequest donors who were annual fund donors?

This information can give you insights for what you might expect from similar donors and prospects.

You must establish clear guidelines to create new permanent funds by establishing a few things, including the fund's purpose, the desired size, and the possible naming opportunities.

Your finance department or controller, working in conjunction with development and your organization's attorney, can provide appropriate accounting and legal records. There should be a standard document to create an endowment fund and an established endowment acceptance process.

You will need to manage active planned giving stewardship that mirrors the stewardship of annual and capital donors. There should be endowment coverage in your written annual report; annual personal contact with the donor, which can include an annual call from a staff person; an annual handwritten thank-you note; a report on the endowment; a planned giving newsletter; and invitations to events on campus. Each planned giving donor should be assigned to a staff person and tracked in the donor management system.

> ### Don't Try to Advise the Donors Yourself
>
> All planned giving prospects should be encouraged to consult their own financial advisors before completing a planned gift with an organization.

Planned Giving Communications

Planned giving should be included as a giving option on your website. Because of the technical nature of planned giving information, it will be worthwhile to consider expanding your website with more detailed information by using a third-party vendor. There are a number of firms that provide this type of service. A click on a link takes the web viewer from your site to an expert's planned giving data on another site. There the viewer can calculate giving amounts and find information specific to the donor's situation. Up-to-date tax law information, gift calculators, retirement calculators, and college calculators are all useful tools provided to engage the prospect in the planning process. Most development officers are not equipped to handle this much financial detail.

Your organization should insert planned giving information into all development communications: annual report, quarterly or monthly magazine, website, endowment brochure/materials or planned giving newsletter.

Endowment communications should use clear messages and should challenge the reader to action. These donors and prospects will merit personal attention. An example of an initial planned giving activity might be to send a special request letter to donors age fifty and above who have given to your organization for the past five years in a row.

A successful planned giving program depends on identifying those elusive

> ### To-Do Lists
>
> There are three groups to consider in your planned giving program:
>
> Those ready to receive an ask
>
> Those that meet the criteria but with whom the organization has not yet established the appropriate relationship
>
> Those with an interest in the organization

planned giving prospects, conducting thorough research, and effectively cultivating them before making the ask. We like to invite all planned giving donors and prospects to all cultivation and recognition events organization wide.

Planned Giving Prospects

A list of planned giving prospects for your organization may include:

◆ People who are well off

◆ People concerned with the receipt of current income

◆ People who may want your organization to exercise management skills over their assets as they grow older

◆ People who are unmarried or widowed

◆ People who are married but without children

◆ People who have tax concerns

◆ People who are significant current donors or past donors

◆ People who are fifty and older

◆ People who have some sort of programmatic tie to your organization or benefited from its services

Do not make the mistake of disregarding *women* as potential prospects for all types of gifts for your organization. Just as planned giving is the fastest growing area of philanthropy today, women are the fastest growing donor population. Statistically they will outlive their spouses, and are more likely to make final dispersion of a family's assets.

These are the important signals to watch for with your own best planned giving prospects:

◆ Donors who have given for five or more years to your organization

◆ Past endowment donors

◆ Current and past board members

◆ Long-term friends, volunteers and staff

◆ Multi-generational families

Select the top ten, twenty or even one hundred prospects that meet more than one of the above categories to focus on in your planned giving program.

Educating Donors about Planned Giving

People make planned gifts because they believe in your organization and are asked to make a planned gift after being properly educated and cultivated. They know you and one or more of your volunteers and staff. They may need tax advantages. The gift may help the donor save money and therefore, the donor can pass on more to heirs. This satisfies the donor's personal obligations and charitable interests at the same time. The planned gift places the investment management responsibilities on others (a bank or investment management firm), which is an important matter for some individuals. Assets can then be managed after death for the benefit of the surviving spouse.

> **Reminder: People Give Because They Are Asked**
>
> People make planned gifts because they believe in your organization's mission and are asked to make a planned gift after being properly educated and cultivated.

While the nonprofit leader does not need to be an expert in planned giving, staff and board members must be trained on planned giving messages. You should develop speed dial relationships with your organization's attorney and wealth managers. Your nonprofit can and should host seminars on estate planning for current donors, their families, constituents, and staff.

Recruit a planned giving committee to assist the development committee, alongside a separate advisory board of professionals in the community. Educate them about your mission and your constituents and establish a planned giving recognition society. You can then solicit planned gifts with confidence.

Building the Endowment beyond Planned Gifts

While planned gifts are the most common way to build an endowment, the funds can also come from other sources. The most common of these is through large gifts of stock. Rather than immediately sell the stock, the board should discuss whether it could better be used to establish the corpus of an endowment. Special consideration must be given to the appropriateness of that stock. For example, a healthcare nonprofit would not want an endowment heavily funded through tobacco stocks.

Older donors may also be interested in designating their *required minimum distributions* (RMDs) to fund an endowment. An RMD is the amount of money that must be withdrawn from an employer-sponsored retirement plan, traditional IRA, SEP, or SIMPLE individual retirement account (IRA) by owners and qualified retirement plan participants of retirement age. For some donors, there are significant tax advantages to designate these RMDs to go directly to a nonprofit.

To Recap

- ◆ Endowment building comes after successful annual and capital fundraising efforts.

- ◆ Planned giving is the best way to build an endowment.

- ◆ There are a few simple steps you can take to begin a planned giving program without breaking your budget.

Chapter Ten

Fundraising Really is for Everyone

IN THIS CHAPTER

···→ Philanthropy is for more than just the wealthy.

···→ Fundraisers have a responsibility to help mold the next generation of philanthropists.

The words "philanthropy" or "philanthropist" most commonly conjure an image of older, wealthy, individuals bestowing large donations in exchange for their names plastered on the side of buildings. However, the root of this word paints a very different image—one we as fundraisers should be cultivating.

Philanthropy is derived from "phil," meaning love, and "anthropos," meaning mankind. In other words, philanthropy is "the love of mankind." According to www.merriam-webster.com, philanthropy is "the giving of money for a purpose or cause benefiting people (or animals) who you don't personally know."

What if one's idea of a philanthropist wasn't limited to the wealthiest among us, but anyone giving of what they have to help others? What if this was taught to children? Imagine the world those children would grow up in and the adults they would become.

The Benefits of Involving Children in Philanthropy

Don't be dismissive of children's spending power. According to *The Kids' Market in the U.S.* (2019), kids aged three to eleven comprise a population subgroup of thirty-six million and have growing influence over family spending of over $20 billion.

Kids Learn Philanthropy

◆ Key findings from Women Give 2018 study include:

◆ Adult children—both sons and daughters—whose parents give to charity are more likely to give to charity.

◆ The relationship between parents' and adult daughters' giving is stronger than the relationship between parents' and adult sons' giving.

◆ The frequency of parents' giving has greater influence on adult daughters' likelihood of giving than it does on adult sons' likelihood of giving.

Young children model the behaviors of the adults around them. According to a 2018 study by the Women's Philanthropy Institute (WPI) at the Indiana University Lilly Family School of Philanthropy, adult children are more likely to give to charitable causes if parents give, especially daughters. If children whose parents are donating to your organization have a higher propensity to become donors themselves, and currently have influence over family spending in other areas, why aren't we helping to influence that behavior towards raising the next generation of philanthropists?

Your nonprofit can offer opportunities for children, teenagers and young adults to be a part of their parents' philanthropy. You may be asking, "Why would I do this? I already have enough work as it is!"

As fundraisers, it is our responsibility to collaborate with parents as they raise the next generation.

Involving children in philanthropy can build real-life competencies like leadership, teamwork, creativity, investment management and financial acumen. It can build empathy and compassion and teaches kids how to make a difference with what they have. One nonprofit both Ailena and Linda have worked with asks children two questions:

"What are your favorite things to do?"

"What breaks your heart?"

Then they help the children find ways to turn their favorite activities into a way to raise money for a nonprofit working to fix the problem they've identified. These children, many for the first time, are being asked where they see a need and then being given the tools to make a difference. That's how you build a philanthropist!

Involving Kids in Campaign Activities

If this is the first time you've considered involving all ages in fundraising for your organization, it might seem overwhelming. Instead of re-inventing the wheel, simply look for ways that you might offer opportunities for the whole family to be involved in your existing activities.

◆ Specifically invite children to accompany their parents to fundraising events such as donor recognition parties or groundbreaking ceremonies.

◆ Invite the children of donors to an official or unofficial National Philanthropy Day event.

◆ Gift a children's book about giving to donors' children with a note of appreciation from the nonprofit in the inside cover.

◆ Feature stories about family giving in a newsletter or on social media.

◆ Establish a giving society for annual donors age twelve and under, thirteen to eighteen and eighteen to twenty-two and cultivate as you would any other donor.

◆ Host a philanthropy club, either onsite or in partnership with a local school.

◆ Invite donors' middle- or high school-aged kids to participate in a thank-a-thon, allowing them to make thank you phone calls and write notes of appreciation to annual donors. Make it fun, have food and offer volunteer hours for those needing them for credit.

◆ Offer career networking events and intentionally invite donors' college and young adult children. Once engaged, you can adopt a peer-to-peer model for soliciting gifts.

Beyond the continued cultivation opportunities this opens up with your existing donors, these children might just grow up and continue supporting your organization throughout their lifetimes.

Engaging this next generation may be even easier now that they have grown up in the digital world. Leverage social media and electronic communication to establish an online relationship between your nonprofit and the youth associated with your philanthropic families. Charitable instincts can be encouraged through technology. Internet-savvy teens can investigate nonprofits through blogs, forums, podcasts, video, etc.

There is no right or wrong age for a student to begin learning about fundraising for nonprofits. Some families discuss giving around the dinner table, and some invite their children to be a part of the solicitation meetings and discuss their decisions as a family. A popular model for Jewish families is for their middle schoolers to donate their bat mitzvah and bar mitzvah gifts to a local charity. These young donors get to learn at an early age about grantmaking decisions and how to choose whom to give to, and why. Ailena once consulted with a family who split their yearly philanthropic budget evenly amongst each member of the family—mother, father, and two teenage boys. They each had to research nonprofits, including reviewing their financial statements, and present to the rest of the family which nonprofits they chose. Each was then responsible for making a gift. A nonprofit closest to the parents could have engaged those teenagers in teaching other families how to implement this model of giving and built a culture of philanthropy amongst an age group often ignored in fundraising.

Stories from the Real World

Over the course of eight years at a healthcare nonprofit, Ailena built a lifelong friendship with a family who were both donors and volunteers. While the father participated in the annual weekend-long cycling fundraiser, the wife and young daughter, Lanie, volunteered. While the nonprofit did not initially have a child-specific volunteer role, they found multiple options that were easily adjusted to allow Lanie to work alongside her mother. As Lanie grew, she followed her parents' example and found ways to use her own talents to raise money for the cause. Ailena remembers attending a benefit concert organized by the parents where Lanie's jewelry was proudly displayed for a donation. Her parents' example of philanthropy, and their partnership with a nonprofit that allowed her participation, taught her that she could make a difference no matter her age.

Linda experienced the beauty and creativity of students in philanthropy during a campaign for a new middle school building. A faculty member coined the idea of having students make speeches about the campaign as part of their required public speaking course. One student gave a tribute to a construction worker. Some were persuasive speeches in support of fundraising; other speeches simply built awareness of the campaign. As the development officer, Linda met with each class and presented the campaign case for support. Students then gave speeches about the middle school campaign with PowerPoint presentations to their classes and then in a public venue. Their audiences ranged from first graders, to board members, to faculty members, and to the entire upper school. Some speeches were given at churches, in homes, at Girl Scout meetings, wherever the student chose. Altogether, 128 speeches were given over a two-year period. The response was terrific. Multiple parents raced into the development office saying their child was making a speech that night and could they please make their campaign gift? These students learned the importance of giving back to their school. They learned the pros and cons of the case, and could explain better than Linda why an upper school family should give to the middle school campaign even though they were not going to personally benefit. The true value of this effort will come in future years when those same students take what they learned and apply it to their own philanthropic endeavors.

Donor Behavior is Established Early

Beyond the ethical aspects of partnering with parents in helping to educate future philanthropists, it's also smart fundraising. In the United States and most western countries, the majority of philanthropic giving comes from those older than fifty-five. This is mostly a function of a household's disposable income. However, donors don't start picking the causes they care about at that age; it occurs much earlier. In the field of consumer marketing, most consumers develop brand preferences and buying behaviors in their late teens and early- to mid-twenties. By the time someone is thirty, they tend to have decided what they "like" and "dislike." At the same time, the foundation of their philanthropic behavior has also been established. Individuals typically determine the causes they care about and are willing to support in this timeframe, even if they don't currently have the disposable income to support those causes at a significant level. It behooves the nonprofit community to include children of all ages in their fundraising and marketing plans. Those children of current donors are already developing the philanthropic interests that will dictate their giving once they mature.

Dave watched this play out while working with two different performing arts organizations. They had different approaches to cultivating young people and these generated drastically different fundraising results.

The first organization, an opera company, viewed their programming as primarily an adult experience. While they had educational programming, it was directed at schools instead of families. There was a general detachment towards children at the evening performances and a coolness towards them in donors' lounges or at galas. Dave encountered the daughter of an elderly, major opera donor at one of their fundraising events. During a polite conversation, he asked if he could host her and her husband at an upcoming performance. She cut him off flatly. "Opera is Mom's thing. She'll support you for whatever years she has left, but that's it. I'd start looking now for a new sugar mama if I were you."

The second organization, a symphony orchestra, went out of its way to create a welcoming environment for kids. It invested in a number of family, educational, and youth engagement programs that made young audience members feel "welcome at the adult table." The chief development officer extended this philosophy to fundraising events and galas. Donors felt their children were always welcome and enjoyed the inclusive atmosphere. At an orchestra fundraiser, Dave spoke with the son of a major donor and board member. The son was now a young adult, early in his career, and had just become a donor. He spoke of how many happy memories from his childhood had included the orchestra. He recalled the honor of meeting the music director and described the experience as making him feel "sophisticated" at a very early age. He confided in Dave he hoped to continue the family tradition of support and involvement and one day serve on the board as well.

Philanthropy is similar to buying behavior in this sense. The first donor's daughter, a woman in her fifties, had already decided she did not enjoy opera and no amount of cultivation was going to convince her otherwise. The second donor's son was included in his father's philanthropic experiences and grew up to be a donor himself.

That is the last, and possibly most valuable, parting thought we can give you. It is far less likely that you are going to convince someone to love your cause or mission late in life. People will decide whether they care about performing arts, historic preservation, or environmental causes long before they have the financial wherewithal to support them. "Development" is the art of developing the future for the organization. That's the ultimate goal of fundraising...for all.

Resources

The Adventures in PhilAnThropy, written by Linda McNay, Del Martin & Ailena Parramore is a children's book that follows young friends Phil, An and Thropy as they embark on an adventure in philanthropy. Perfect for reading aloud to a group of young philanthropists or gifting to donors, the book is available on Amazon or at www.ourfundraisingsearch.com.

Indiana University Lilly Family School of Philanthropy increases the understanding of philanthropy and improves its practice worldwide through critical inquiry, interdisciplinary research, teaching, training and civic engagement. A number of resources and articles are available discussing the topic of children in philanthropy.

(https://philanthropy.iupui.edu and https://blog.philanthropy.iupui.edu)

Local community foundations also have a number of programs focusing on intergenerational philanthropy and transition of wealth.

To Recap

Students will have the capacity to give later in life. The important thing is to develop the inclination to give as early as possible. If children, both young and old, are given the opportunity to engage with your organization in a meaningful way, they will develop an appreciation for the worthiness of your cause and the payoff in the future could be significant.

Afterword

Linda Gets the Last Word

This book is both a labor of love and a challenge among the three of us. Back in 2020, when the world was quarantined and Our Fundraising Search had to reinvent how we did business, we had time to think about how the COVID-19 pandemic was going to impact nonprofits. We also recognized that we had something to say—well, some things to say—that might help nonprofits navigate the uncertainties ahead.

This is the fifth fundraising book I have written or co-written. We've got a good bit of experience in the field, which we document in this book. This book is just the latest in the long and ever-evolving trajectory of our company, Our Fundraising Search.

Among other things, Our Fundraising Search helps nonprofits find and keep good development officers. We have around 1,200 resumes on hand on any given day, we interview candidates constantly, and we help them find the jobs of their dreams. While the nationwide average tenure of a development officer is fourteen to eighteen months, our placements stay an average of forty-three months, or three times longer. As of the writing of this book we have conducted more than sixty searches since I founded the company in 2013. Our sweet spot for clients has been small- to medium-sized nonprofits that may not have human resources departments.

Our business came about because our clients were having trouble finding experienced fundraisers. At the time, I was working at a large consulting firm and my boss knew of my background in human resources. I have an MBA in human resources and long before I was a fundraiser myself, I served as an H. R. director in a major hotel chain. Our goal was for me to conduct five searches a year in addition to running capital campaigns. In ten months, I had done ten searches. I was so excited! I knew someone should be doing this full time. My boss did not want to be in the search business, but he did not care if I was. So, Our Fundraising Search was born.

Since then, everything we have done has been on behalf of and at the request of our clients. Search has turned out to be only half of our business. If it has to do with fundraising, we can help.

We created "Walk with the Consultant" to engage groups of job hunters, because we had so much interest, we could no longer meet one on one with everyone who was keen on joining the profession. To this day, we are available for a regular monthly walk and occasionally on demand to discuss job interest in the area.

We now offer interim staffing because our clients asked for that service. "Linda, can you write this grant? Linda, can you run this event while you are conducting our director of development search?" We used to say no, but now we say yes. We collect resumes of those individuals who only want to work part-time or gig work and we place them temporarily, and everybody wins.

At Our Fundraising Search, we are committed to diversity and to providing our clients a well-rounded slate of top candidates. Early on, we joined with The Association of Fundraising Professionals (AFP) in serving as mentors in its diversity fellows program. Every year, I get to mentor one individual, get to know a dozen more, and stay in touch with them. In addition, we provide the AFP's year-end program on resume writing, interviewing, and finding the next development role. We also partner with African American Development Officer Network (AADO) to provide a more diverse set of candidates for our clients.

In partnership with AFP, we have taken our children's book into the classroom with the Atlanta chapter's Philanthropy in the Classroom (PIC) program. AFP Atlanta launched the PIC program in 2009 to introduce to elementary children the concept of philanthropy. The program's growth includes a strong partnership with the Kiwanis Club, a National Philanthropy Day Presenting Sponsor. The children's artwork created through this program is displayed on National Philanthropy Day. AFP volunteers have worked with hundreds of children in multiple elementary schools throughout Atlanta through this initiative. We wrote the resource book for them because there was not a satisfactory one.

We offer fundraising coaching to individuals because our clients asked for it. We conduct CEO searches because our clients asked for it. During the pandemic, we added strategic planning to our portfolio and a grantwriting team. We thought we were in the search business, but as it happens, we are in the fundraising business. We thought we were Atlanta based, but after COVID pushed virtual meetings into the mainstream, we are now national—to date we have worked in twelve different states. Beginning in 2021, we offer twenty-one different fundraising consulting services, wherever our clients are located.

I tell you all of this to illustrate this point: fundraising is a complex and ever-changing field, so our company is on an ever-changing trajectory to keep up with (and occasionally influence) the trajectory of the industry. This book, while more comprehensive than my others, will not be the last word on the topic.

I wrote my first fundraising book on school fundraising because I had worked at my kids' school and schools were a major part of my network. I kept meeting with other headmasters and repeating myself. So I finally wrote it all down for them. Weeks later, *Fundraising for Schools* was published.

Fundraising for Museums was published in 2015 and shared with our colleagues at the Building Museums Conference in Washington. We are pleased to report our books are being used as required reading in college and university arts programs today.

Fundraising for Churches with Sarah Matthews was published in 2017. We also created an accompanying online course. We believe churches need to raise money like other nonprofits if they want to continue to grow and thrive.

Each of these resources is a basic "how to" fundraising book packed with tried-and-true principles. The stories we tell vary based on the audience. Our books are for nonprofit leaders from CEOs to board chairs and board members, to staff whose jobs may or may not be fundraising. I am told these resources are helpful and down to earth, and a jumping off point for those who may be new to the profession.

Our clients in healthcare, environmental causes, parks and other fields have asked us for their own "how to" books. As always wanting to help, but not personally sure how many more books I had in me, my distinguished colleagues, Dave Paule and Ailena Parramore and I have teamed together to bring you one more volume, *Fundraising for All*.

The most important thought I would like to leave you with is this: fundraising is important. Nonprofits can't execute their missions without revenue, and nonprofits can't raise revenue without fundraisers. If you are a fundraiser, what you do is valuable and meaningful. We are grateful you are there to do it. And I am grateful that you cared enough to pick up this book.

Linda Wise McNay, PhD

June, 2021

Atlanta, Ga

Index

You've been offered a chief executive role with a new organization. Congratulations! Of course, now you need to know what questions to ask to determine if you really want the job. In **The CEO's Due Diligence Handbook,** David M. Paule helps you compile your list of questions for your hiring organization, and gives you insightful perspectives on what their answers should look like, not to mention what could be wrong if they don't.

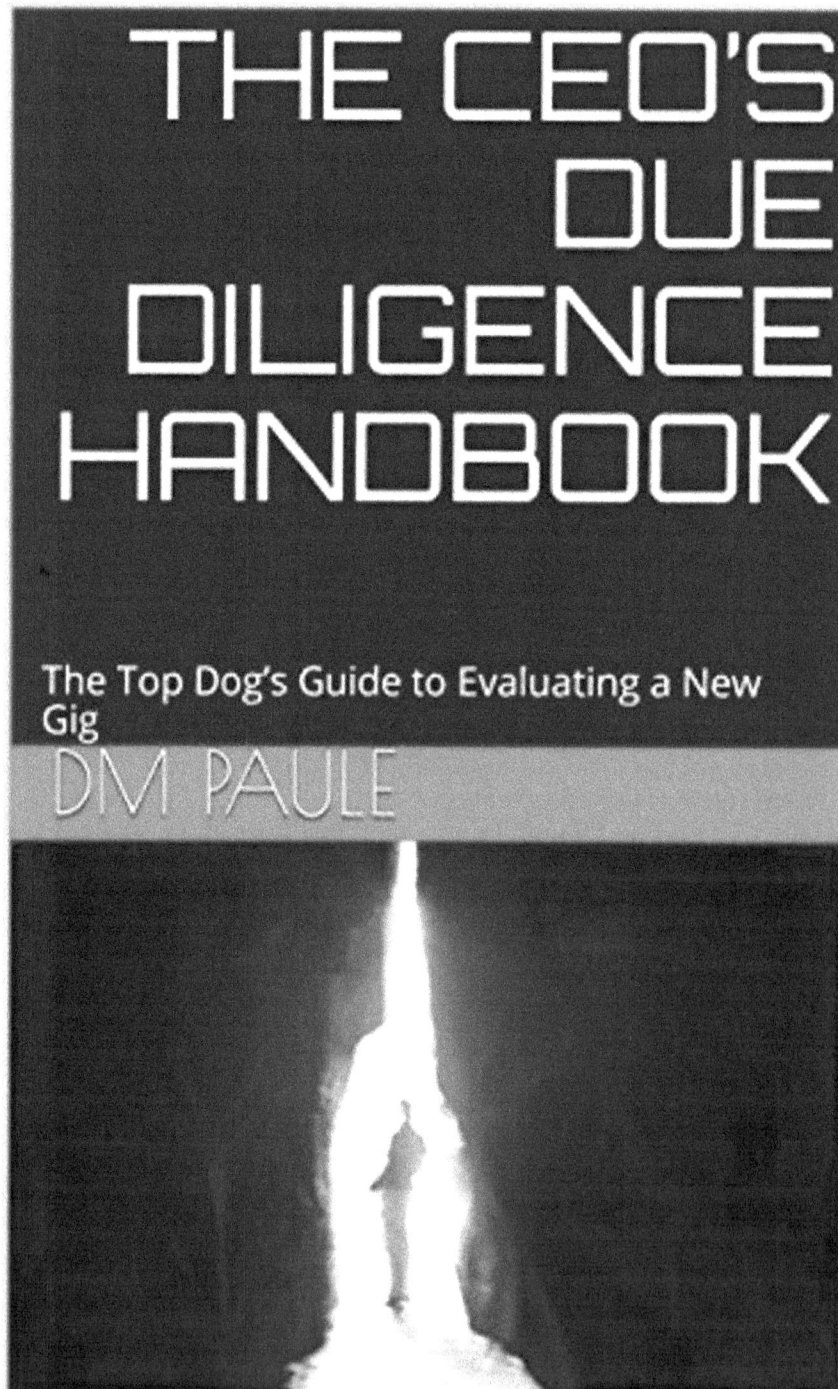

THE CEO'S DUE DILIGENCE HANDBOOK

The Top Dog's Guide to Evaluating a New Gig

DM PAULE

The Adventures of PhilAnThropy introduces readers to young friends Phil, An and Thropy as they embark on an adventure in philanthropy upon realizing their new friend needs a special chairlift to enjoy the neighborhood pool. This wonderful resource for parents will inspire children of all ages that contributions both big and small can truly make a lasting impact.

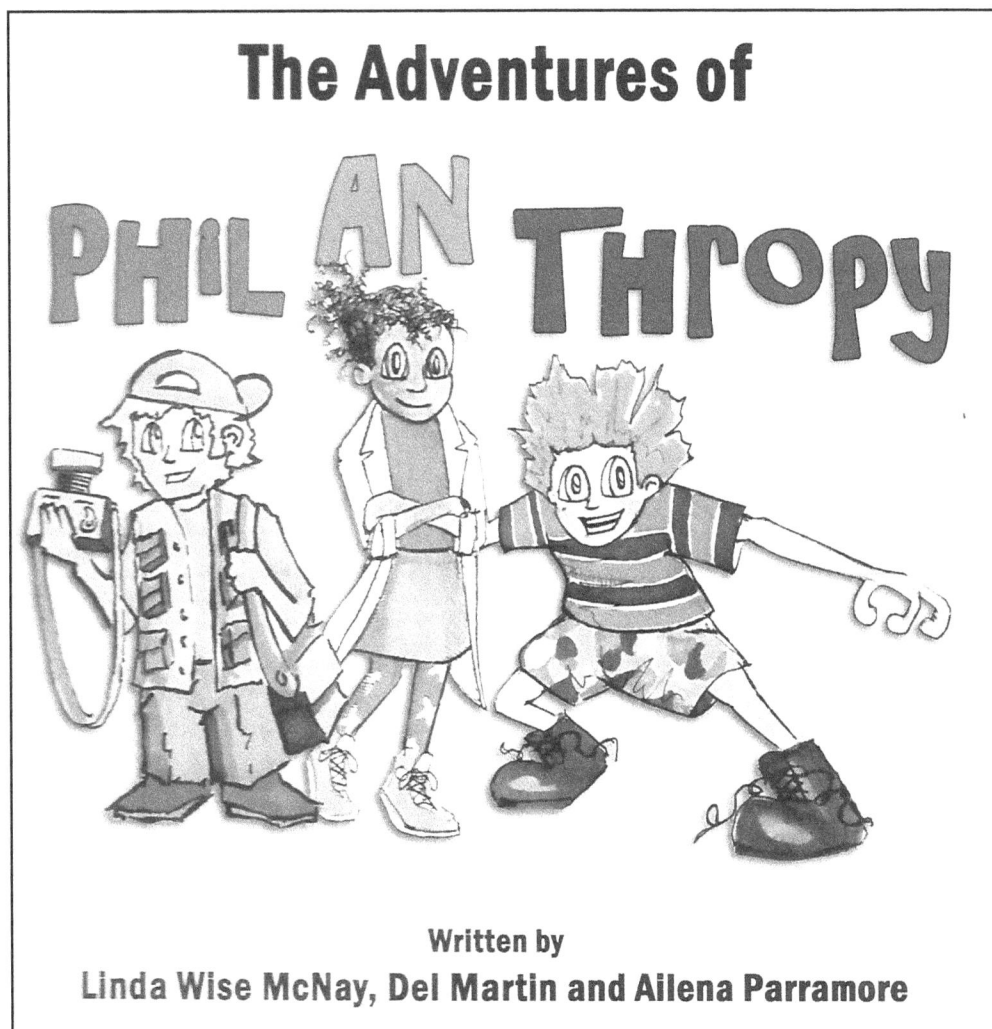

The Adventures of

PHiL AN THRoPY

Written by
Linda Wise McNay, Del Martin and Ailena Parramore

Being a head of a museum is both challenging and rewarding work. Museum leaders and those who aspire to the role are expected to engage donors and members and raise money effectively; yet, most have received little or no training or support in advancement. In **Fundraising for Museums: 8 Keys to Success Every Museum Leader Should Know,** veteran fundraising consultant Linda Wise McNay demystifies fundraising for museum leaders.

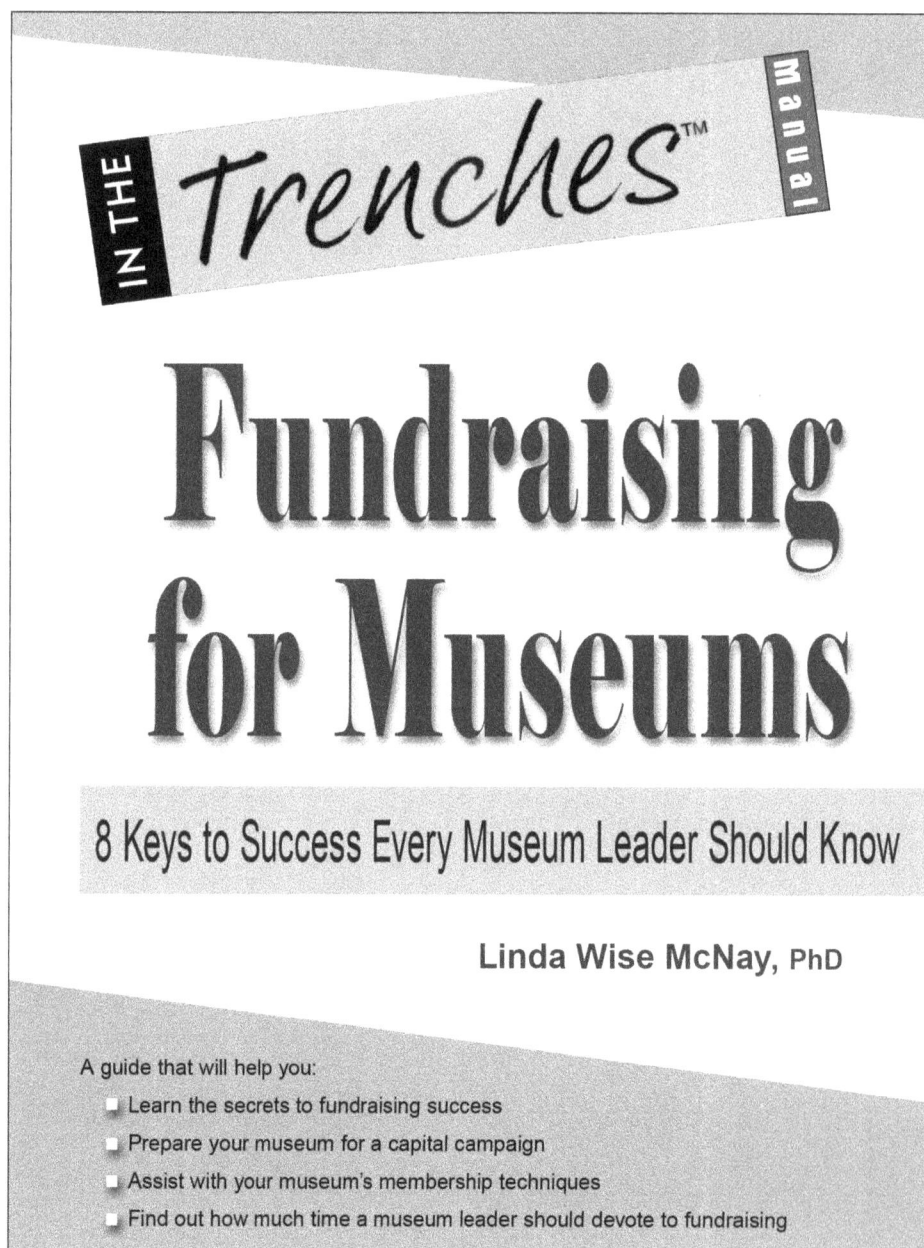

IN THE

Trenches™

Manual

Fundraising for Museums

8 Keys to Success Every Museum Leader Should Know

Linda Wise McNay, PhD

A guide that will help you:

- Learn the secrets to fundraising success
- Prepare your museum for a capital campaign
- Assist with your museum's membership techniques
- Find out how much time a museum leader should devote to fundraising

Fundraising for Churches: 12 Keys to Success Every Church Leader Should Know was written because your church or faith-based organization needs to raise money, including annual operating support as well as capital and endowment funds for building and maintenance.

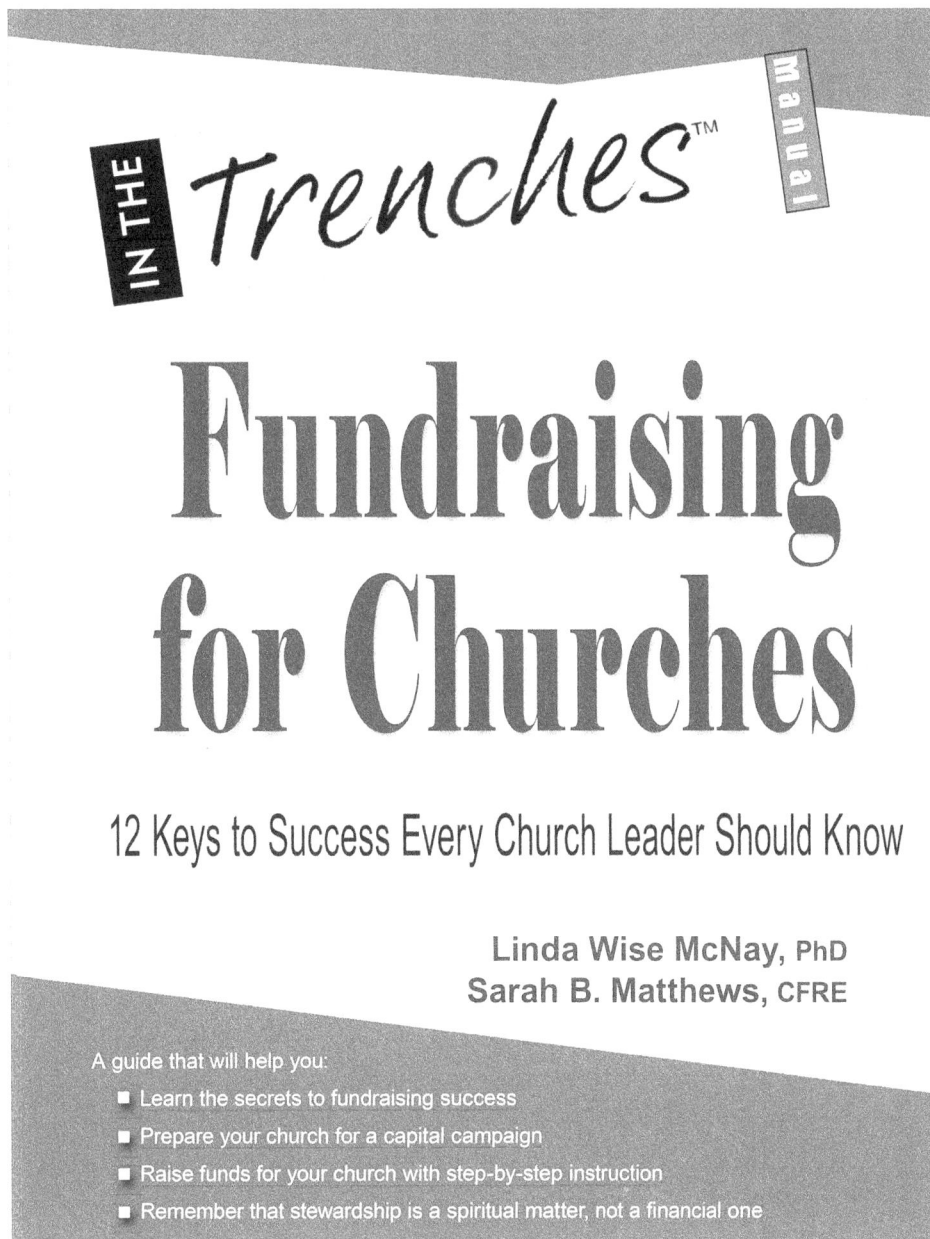

IN THE *Trenches*™ Manual

Fundraising for Churches

12 Keys to Success Every Church Leader Should Know

Linda Wise McNay, PhD
Sarah B. Matthews, CFRE

A guide that will help you:

- Learn the secrets to fundraising success
- Prepare your church for a capital campaign
- Raise funds for your church with step-by-step instruction
- Remember that stewardship is a spiritual matter, not a financial one

Heads of school and those who aspire to the role are expected to engage alumni and parents and raise money effectively; yet, most have received little or no training or support in advancement. In **Fundraising for Schools: 8 Keys to Success Every Head of School Should Know,** veteran fundraising consultant Linda Wise McNay demystifies fundraising for school leaders.

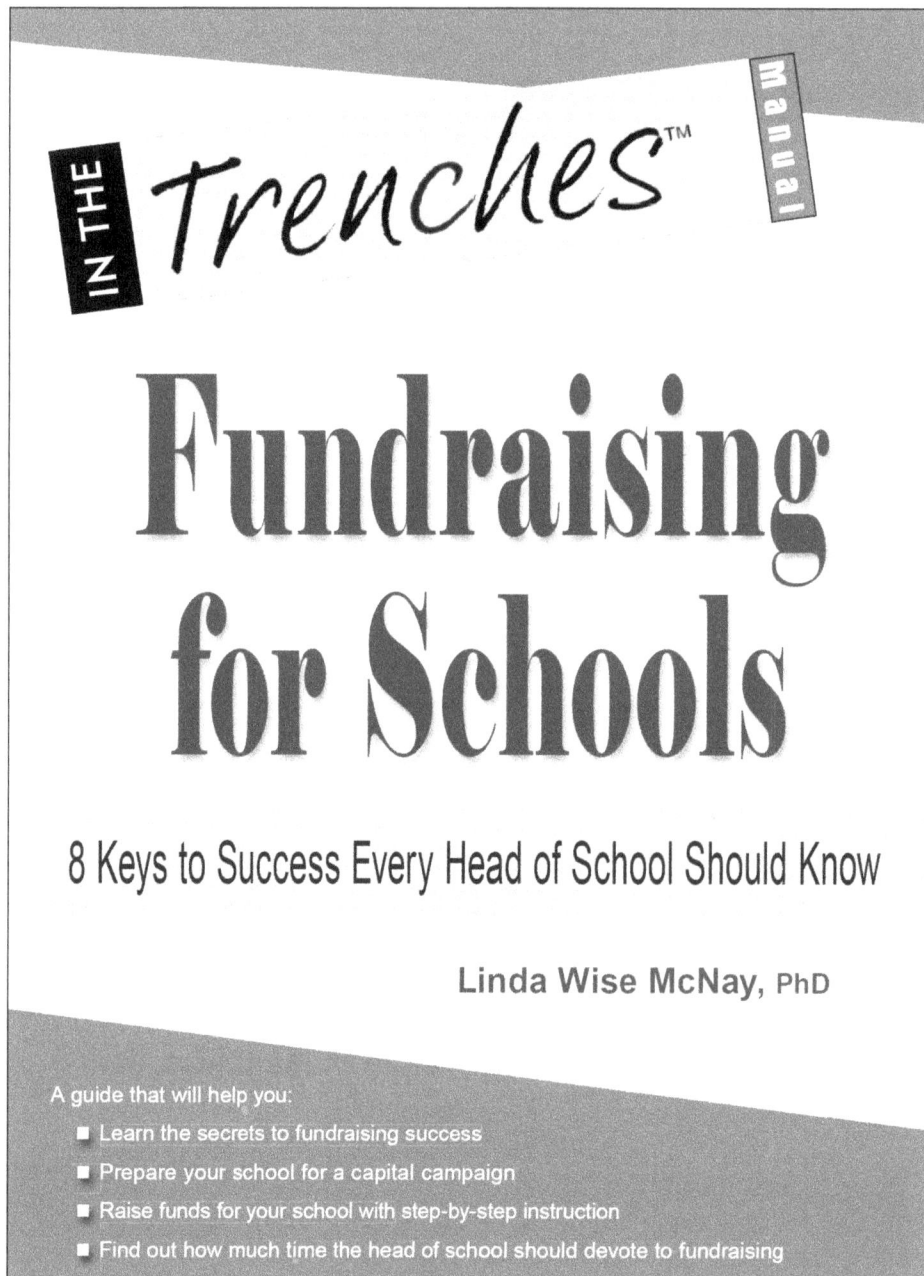

IN THE *Trenches*™ Manual

Fundraising for Schools

8 Keys to Success Every Head of School Should Know

Linda Wise McNay, PhD

A guide that will help you:
- Learn the secrets to fundraising success
- Prepare your school for a capital campaign
- Raise funds for your school with step-by-step instruction
- Find out how much time the head of school should devote to fundraising

Learn more about these books at ourfundraisingschool.com or buy them at amazon.com.